BIRDS IN YOUR BACKYARD

Typical native birds in their habitats

By
VIRGINIA S. EIFERT
with revisions by
MILTON D. THOMPSON

Illustrations by
THE AUTHOR
and
ROBERT G. LARSON

POPULAR SCIENCE SERIES VOL. II

Illinois State Museum
Springfield, Illinois
1986

1986
ISSN 0360-0297
ISBN 0-89792-031-7
Printed by Authority of the State of Illinois
(P.O. 53990—2M—6/86)
1st edition, 1941
2nd printing, 1945
2nd edition, 1967
2nd printing, 1986

PREFACE

"Birds in Your Backyard," first published in 1941 and reprinted in 1945, was designated for a new printing this year. Virginia Eifert was in the process of revising the text when, in June 1966, her untimely death brought an end to the flow from the pen that so readably expressed her insight, enjoyment and understanding of the world about her. It is with considerable trepidation that I add my prosaic prose to her lyrical manner of expression as I undertake to update and supplement the information she has given.

Bird populations are dynamic and variable as they are affected by ever-changing pressures in the environment, especially those created by our increasing population and its mobility, the diversified uses of the land, and the development of new concepts in wildlife management. The additions and revisions made here reflect changes which have occurred during the twenty-five years since the book was first printed as well as certain other facets of bird life that may be of interest.

Some of the pages remain exactly as they were. On some, sentences have been added or deleted, and a few are essentially rewritten (pages 42, 44, 48, 56, 58, 62, 106, 116, and 192). One new page was added to include three white herons now in Illinois (page 26).

I hope the reader will find my efforts acceptable and helpful — and realize that I, too, had fallen under the spell of Virginia Eifert's personality and literary skill and, above all, her friendship. I approach this task with no desire to destroy her work but, rather, to prevent its obsolescence.

May 1967   MILTON D. THOMPSON
Museum Director

PREFACE TO THE 1986 REPRINTING

Because the work of Virginia Eifert continues to remain popular, this 1967 edition of *Birds in your Backyard* has been reprinted. There are minor alterations. Bird names change, and the current common names recognized by the American Ornithological Union have been added in parentheses to the illustration labels. Elsewhere, the common names used by Virginia Eifert have been retained.

The status of many species has also changed, but for historical reasons the original text as revised by Milton D. Thompson in the 1967 edition has not been changed. The same is true of the locality descriptions. Birders today will immediately recognize changes in the Illinois habitats described by the author.

Milton D. Thompson contributed the text for the herons on page 27 and Robert D. Larson executed the accompanying plate.

NANCY M. WELLS
Editor

ACKNOWLEDGMENTS

The author is indebted to Dr. Arthur A. Allen of Cornell University for a critical reading of the manuscript and valuable advice on text and drawings; to Mr. Alexander Dawes Dubois for his able and constructive criticism of the illustrations; and to Dr. Frank M. Chapman of the American Museum of Natural History for his kind permission to use certain phrases from his book, "Handbook of Birds."

Members of the Bird Group and other members of the Springfield Nature League who, over a period of years, have recorded their findings among local birds directly or indirectly have added much to the value of this book.

And to all those whose assistance and friendship have made possible the pursuit of birds in Sangamon County, in the Illinois State Museum, and elsewhere in Illinois, the author owes a deep debt of gratitude.

March 15, 1941   VIRGINIA S. EIFERT

INTRODUCTION

B IRDS IN YOUR BACKYARD is a series of word and brush impressions of the birds of Sangamon County, Central Illinois, and the Illinois State Museum, about the places in which they live, and their association with trees and lakes and open fields. A checklist of birds of an area tells a concise tale of its bird population; but such a list and story can be only temporary. Changing conditions in climate, in the coming of artificial lakes, and in the growth of cities already have changed the old bird lists of this territory, and no one knows what other changes may take place tomorrow or next year. New birds—those not listed before for this region—are becoming a common occurence, so that one cannot say with assurance that a certain bird can never be seen in Illinois. There is no way to tell how frequently they may be seen in the future, nor what other unusual creatures may come winging into the area.

But there are dozens of commoner birds that return each year with regularity to the accustomed haunts. When one of these is seen, look at it carefully as long as its wildness permits. Hastily jot down its main points, the size, the prominent colors, the large areas of light and dark. Note especially the shape of the beak because this one feature alone will tell much about the group of birds to which it belongs.

At this point there might be innumerable keys into which one could painstakingly delve in search of the bird in question. But aside from museum specimens, a good picture is a practical method of identifying the bird. And one of the best ways to identify it is to start at the beginning of the bird book and thumb through it, page after page, until a bird is found which has the right markings. Purposely the entire book may have to be examined. As other birds are found, this occurs many times, until one soon comes to know the approximate location of bird groups in the book and can save himself time by eliminating the water birds and game birds when the bird in question is undoubtedly neither. Meanwhile the volume acquires that comfortable, well-used look which is the grace of useful books and besides, and far more important, it has given one a memory of many birds. To look often at bird pictures is a good habit. Each bird has its own pattern and at least one good distinguishing mark, and these become so fixed in the memory that a new bird in the wild is not entirely strange; the bird-seeker almost knows where to find it in the book and knows certainly whether it is a warbler or a finch, can tell a plover from a sandpiper without much trouble, can tell a hawk from an owl merely by looking at the shape of the head. And when the family is determined, it usually is a simple matter to identify the species.

There are many ways to enjoy birds. To some, the pictures in a book are enough for the moment, either for those who once went afield for birds or for those who may never be able to go birding. To others, the live birds out-of-doors are first in importance, and the book is merely a stepping-stone conveniently placed along the way to identification.

And there is still another sort of bird book—the Museum. Dr. Frank M. Chapman says in his "Birds of Eastern North America" —"If you would 'name the birds without a gun', by all means first visit the Museum, and, with textbook in hand, study those species which you have previously found are to be looked for near your home. This preliminary introduction will serve to ripen your acquaintance in the field."

Museum exhibits today may not show hundreds of bird specimens displayed row after row like a textbook illustrated with mounted birds; but you may be surprised at the great variety of birds included in the exhibits, especially in the natural habitat scenes. Here you must seek them out among the tree branches, shrubs, and ground cover. They are not as elusive as in the out-of-doors; for, once you locate them, they will not fly away.

If you do not find in the displays the bird in which you are especially interested, the Museum curators can take you to the laboratory where most native species can be studied in their varied plumages.

However, it is the wild birds which are best of all. Neither Museum nor book can completely take their place. These are only substitutes for life, and life flutters out there in the garden, in the clover field, in the swamp, in the meadow, in the elms along the street. Birds are there, and one must go there to look at living, flitting things. With binoculars or opera glasses, a bird guide, and clothing that is not too bright, go out to the birds. The glasses need not be at all costly; unaided eyes will do. Quiet, deliberate movements, patience, a love of wild things, and the habit of melting into one's surroundings until the birds have forgotten about the intruder are perhaps best of all equipment for birding.

The best time of day to see birds is early morning when they are very active, not too shy, and singing at their best. By late morning they are drowsy, and many of them hunt a secluded spot and take a siesta until midafternoon. Then there is another hunt for food to tide them through the night, and again they sing.

And so birding narrows itself chiefly to these few points: Own a bird book in which you can make notes, especially the dates and places where each bird was first identified. If possible, use field glasses or opera glasses, but don't feel that birding is impossible if neither is available. Visit the Illinois State Museum, or any other museum where bird collections are shown, and ramble among the cases, not once but many times. Then go out and see birds. This may mean only your own backyard where a birdbath will attract more birds than may be supposed until a careful count is made of daily visitors.

Note each new bird, its main marks, size, and general shape. Run it down in the bird book, put down the date, either in a notebook or in the bird book itself. And then seek another bird . . . and another . . . and still another. Soon there will grow an acquaintance-list of birds which is one of the finest satisfactions of this workaday world. The door is open—the birds are waiting. Good hunting!

THE BREADLINE

IN WINTER it is good to see small birds flitting in the bare bushes, picking seeds from weeds left in the shivering garden, birds hunting for a livelihood in stubble, grass plot, and trees. It is these birds whose bravery and courage touch the heart. Their life and exuberance seem unhampered by want or cold and their enthusiastic personalities unconsciously ignite one's own enthusiasm. They satisfy a thirst for life and color; they make a busy day more lovely, take away the pain of loneliness, dispel the gloom of winter clouds.

Winter is a serious matter to the birds, and to the people who like to have them in their gardens. In summer it was sufficient to supply a pool of fresh water daily; food was everywhere to be had for the pecking, and human beings need have little concern over the supply. Winter is a different problem. Yet it is one of the easiest things in the world to bring birds closer, to keep them in gardens and trees. Birds welcome friendliness, and food in severe weather soon brings them flocking.

Only two things are needed: first, a place, and second, the correct food. Almost any kind of feeding stand will do—a cleared foot of ground that admits alike the plebeian and the aristocrat, an elaborate commercial stand which revolves in the wind and admits only the elect, or a window shelf fastened outside the dining room or kitchen windows. Some shelves may be merely a board supported by a couple of chains or braces and placed at window level. There is also the table type—a board or tray nailed to a post. Often an old table has served a varied host and is more successful in bringing a large number and variety of birds than the window-sill tray whose nearness to the house often keeps the shyer birds away.

Place and equipment, then, aren't one's greatest concern. What is really important is the kind of food. Birds have individual tastes, definite cut-and-dried habits of eating which are ages old. Most birds are constructed to eat certain foods—there are seed-eaters, insect-eaters, fruit-eaters. One may eat only grain, another only

8

insects. The shape of the beak has a great deal to do with this: a long, slender beak can't crack corn, a heavy, corn-cracker beak can't dig into a crevice after a spider's eggs.

Of all the foods which might be fed to the hungry throng waiting patiently outside the door, perhaps that old standby chicken-feed, or "scratch," especially that ground for baby chicks, is best liked by the largest number of birds. Others listed in order of preference by the most birds are as follows:

Suet—a little lasts a long time.

Whole corn—scattered ears picked up along the highway will do.

Bread—crusts, crumbs, dry bread.

Fruit—especially chopped apples, rotten or sound.

Sunflower seeds—a luxury, but the birds love them.

Raw peanuts or peanut butter.

Put the corn, crumbs, or fruit, or all of them together, on the feeding stand, on the windowsill, or on the ground, whichever sort of place has been provided. On a tree trunk near the house tie a large chunk of suet well out of reach of dogs. Fasten it firmly with a heavy cord so that it can't be pulled loose either by the weight of the bird perching on it or by one pulling morsels from below.

If you use a suet basket, dip it in melted suet to protect the birds from damage by the raw, cold metal in midwinter. The suet might also be melted and poured into holes bored into a section of a tree limb which is then hung from a branch—a good thing, but perhaps no more effective than the ordinary method.

It may take several days before anything but sparrows comes to the handout. Then, one day, perhaps a flash of red will fly past the window and stop for a bite of corn. A cardinal. It picks up a hard grain and cracks it in that big red beak while the beggar-sparrows sit about and pick up the crumbs. The cardinal is lovely out there in the snow; and although it may have been seen a dozen times in summer, there is a new sense of joy in this, the first of a thousand birds which will come to dine.

More than that, it will have been proved that there is now a workable feeding stand. Gratifyingly, the food disappears, but it is a simple matter to pour a cupful of feed on to the stand and replenish the bird station every morning as the breadline increases. They'll sit about in the trees and bushes and cheep impatiently if breakfast is late.

On the suet tree one day there may also be a visitor—a small black and white bird that pecks busily at the suet and returns again

9

and again throughout the day. The downy woodpecker is often the only suet-eater in town; yet there are others less frequently seen which must depend upon insect eggs and sleeping insects for their meat diet, until one day they find this generous handout of suet.

Midmorning is best for watching birds feeding. A bird's daily winter program begins with the late rising of the winter sun and continues with the immediate need for breakfast after the long, foodless night. In cold weather this breakfast is highly important. A bird's body temperature is normally around 110 degrees, and to maintain it in severe weather the bird has only two means—extra warm feathers which fluff out to make dead-air spaces that hold heat; and food which the body turns into heat and energy. Birds will not freeze if they have enough food. No day is too bitter if they are able to maintain their body heat.

Therefore, as soon as they waken they begin their hunt for something to eat. From the hours of eight until about eleven in the morning, the feeding stand has its most constant and interesting attendance. From about noon until three o'clock the birds find a sheltered spot in the sun, fluff out their feathers, and doze for a while. It is during this afternoon siesta that the feeding stand may go unoccupied, until the birds come again for food to tide them through the long, cold night. Thus, there is no need for anything elaborate nor any special way of attracting birds. If the food is there, the birds will come.

A feeding stand is as simple as that. Try it.

BIRDS IN YOUR BACKYARD

NO MATTER WHERE YOU LIVE, there are birds. Cities have them, even among skyscrapers. Gardens have them, even among the petunias. So have city streets, parks, villages, country roads, and fields. Even the open sky has its birds.

The birds are there. All that remains is for human eyes to see them, hunt them out, enjoy them, watch for them season after season. A familiarity with birds, few or many, is a possession which nothing can mar. It is good to have memory of birds singing in splendid early morning chorus in May; an intimate glimpse of a shy, wild bird unconscious of human presence is a priceless possession. The pursuit of birds fits well into other things—into the hiker's trail, the fisherman's lakes, into the haunts of the swimmer, the camper, the farmer, the motorist, the man walking to work every day, the woman looking from her kitchen window, the gardener planting seeds, the child in the schoolyard. Birds are everywhere.

For birds are no respecters of boundaries. In a yard only a few blocks from the business district of the capital city, nearly one hundred kinds of birds have been reported in garden bushes, bird pool, and feeding stand. Migrants that pass over stop for a while; winter visitors explore tree trunks or dine on cracked corn; summer birds often nest in the garden. Birds from the lake and other high-flying birds pass through the upper sky.

A city garden is a small oasis offering greenery, water, and food, and birds invariably find it. Yet a backyard may be of wider scope. The country dweller has vaster possibilities in his woodlot, his pasture pond, his sunny upland where the blackberries grow, and in his own gardens and barns. The suburban resident has a chance at birds that venture in from the edge of town, where fields meet gardens or where streets merge with parks.

Here birds are doubly abundant; a wooded city park often has more birds per year than a wooded area of equal size farther away from civilization, and a cemetery is noted for numbers. Folk who live beside a lake have the peculiar advantages of a different sort of environment. The large artificial lakes which have been set down as if by a magician's hand in gentle valleys of the prairies have brought birds that before must have flown high without stopping. Now many months of the year see hordes of ducks and geese and other water birds, even an occasional flock of rare blue and snow geese. Folk whose backyards are partly lake water find coots and grebes, hooded mergansers and goldeneyes, and perhaps ten thousand mallards within sight of the kitchen windows. Duck hawks, ospreys, and eagles fly past in winter; in spring and summer there may be gulls and terns, egrets and great blue herons, in exciting quantity and never-ending variation. A backyard by a lake is one of the best places for a sight of unusual birds.

The following birds have been reported within the city of Springfield, either flying over or at rest in the business district:

Great Blue Heron	Barn Owl
Canada Goose	Common Nighthawk
Mallard	Chimney Swift
Double-crested Cormorant	Ruby-throated Hummingbird
Sharp-shinned Hawk	Horned Lark
Red-tailed Hawk	Purple Martin
Turkey Vulture	Tree Swallow
Sparrow Hawk	Cedar Waxwing
Pigeon Hawk	Starling
Killdeer	House Sparrow
Herring Gull	Common Grackle
Ring-billed Gull	Redwinged Blackbird
Screech Owl	American Goldfinch

The person who lives within a few blocks of the business district may watch backyard trees and shrubbery in order to add these birds to the preceding list:

Yellow-billed Cuckoo	Brown Creeper
Black-billed Cuckoo	House Wren
Yellow-shafted Flicker	Bewick's Wren
Red-headed Woodpecker	Brown Thrasher
Downy Woodpecker	Catbird
Yellow-bellied Sapsucker	Mockingbird
Great Crested Flycatcher	Robin
Blue Jay	Hermit Thrush
Black-capped Chickadee	Swainson's Thrush
Tufted Titmouse	Veery

Ruby-crowned Kinglet
Golden-crowned Kinglet
Warbling Vireo
Black-and-white Warbler
Golden-winged Warbler
Tennessee Warbler
Nashville Warbler
Yellow Warbler
Magnolia Warbler
Myrtle Warbler
Black-throated Green Warbler
Blackburnian Warbler

Chestnut-sided Warbler
Blackpoll Warbler
Pine Warbler
Ovenbird
Waterthrush
Yellowthroat
American Redstart
Baltimore Oriole
Cardinal
Rose-breasted Grosbeak
White-throated Sparrow
White-crowned Sparrow

He who lives along the outer portions of town and can include park and pond within his backyard may add the following birds to the foregoing list for a total of what may be found in such an area:

Pied-billed Grebe
Green Heron
Black Duck
Pintail
Gadwall
American Widgeon
Blue-winged Teal
Lesser Scaup
Bufflehead
Cooper's Hawk
Bobwhite
Ring-necked Pheasant
American Coot
American Woodcock
Common Snipe
Semipalmated Sandpiper
Pectoral Sandpiper
Spotted Sandpiper
Mourning Dove
Barred Owl
Great Horned Owl
Belted Kingfisher
Red-bellied Woodpecker
Hairy Woodpecker
Eastern Kingbird

Eastern Phoebe
Eastern Wood Pewee
Yellow-bellied Flycatcher
Traill's Flycatcher
Least Flycatcher
Bank Swallow
Rough-winged Swallow
Barn Swallow
Common Crow
White-breasted Nuthatch
Red-breasted Nuthatch
Winter Wren
Carolina Wren
Wood Thrush
Eastern Bluebird
Blue-gray Gnatcatcher
White-eyed Vireo
Red-eyed Vireo
Solitary Vireo
Yellow-throated Vireo
Blue-winged Warbler
Black-throated Blue Warbler
Cape May Warbler
Cerulean Warbler
Bay-breasted Warbler

Prairie Warbler

Palm Warbler

Connecticut Warbler

Mourning Warbler

Hooded Warbler

Wilson's Warbler

Canada Warbler

Yellow-breasted Chat

Eastern Meadowlark

Orchard Oriole

Scarlet Tanager

Summer Tanager

Indigo Bunting

Dickcissel

Purple Finch

Common Redpoll

Pine Siskin

Rufous-sided Towhee

Grasshopper Sparrow

Henslow's Sparrow

Vesper Sparrow

Slate-colored Junco

Tree Sparrow

Chipping Sparrow

Field Sparrow

Fox Sparrow

Swamp Sparrow

Song Sparrow

The total species of birds to be seen in city backyards is unbelievably large. From the smoky city sky above railroad yard and busy street to the open lake and the wild forest along the river, there are birds to be had for the finding. No matter where you live, there are birds in your backyard.

FOR ADDITIONAL READING

ALLEN, ARTHUR A. Book of Bird Life. Princeton, N. J., Van Nostrand, 2nd ed., 1961.

BLACHLY, LOU, and JENKS, R. Naming the Birds at a Glance. New York, Knopf, 1963.

CHAPMAN, FRANK M. Handbook of Birds of Eastern North America. New York, Dover, 1967.

COLLINS, HENRY H., and BOYAJIAN, N. Familiar Garden Birds of America. New York, Harper, 1965.

DAVISON, VERNE E. Attracting Birds from the Prairies to the Atlantic. New York, Crowell, 1966.

FORBUSH, EDWARD HOWE, and MAY, JOHN R. Natural History of the Birds of Eastern and Central North America. Boston, Houghton Mifflin, 1939.

EIFERT, VIRGINIA S. Invitation to Birds. Illinois State Museum, Springfield, Story of Illinois Series, No. 5, 4th printing, 1953.

GOVAN, ADA CLAPHAM. Wings at My Window. N. Y., MacMillan, 1940.

HICKEY, JOSEPH J. A Guide to Bird Watching. New York, Oxford, 1943.

KIERAN, JOHN. Introduction to Birds. Garden City, N. Y., Doubleday.

LANSDOWNE, JAMES F. Birds of the Northern Forests. Boston, Houghton Mifflin, 1966.

MATHEWS, F. SCHUYLER. Field Book of Wild Birds and Their Music. New York, Putnam's Sons, 1966.

MCELROY, THOMAS P. The New Handbook of Attracting Birds. New York, Knopf, 1960.

MCKENNEY, MARGARET. Birds in the Garden and How to Attract Them. New York, Grosset.

NATIONAL GEOGRAPHIC SOCIETY. Song and Garden Birds of North America. (Includes phonograph records of bird calls.)

NICE, MARGARET. Watcher at the Nest. New York, Dover, 1966.

PEARSON, T. GILBERT. Birds of America. Garden City, N. Y., Doubleday, 1936.

PETERSON, ROGER TORY. Field Guide to the Birds. Boston, Houghton Mifflin, 1947.

PETERSON, ROGER TORY. How to Know the Birds. Boston, Houghton Mifflin, 1962.

PETTINGILL, O. S., editor. Birdwatcher's America. New York, McGraw-Hill, 1965.

PETTINGILL, O. S. Guide to Bird Finding East of the Mississippi. New York, Oxford, 1953.

POUGH, RICHARD H. Audubon Bird Guides: Land Birds; Water Birds. 2 Vols. Garden City, N. Y., Doubleday, 1949 and 1951.

ROBBINS, CHANDLER, BRUUN, BERTEL, and ZIMM, HERBERT. Birds of North America: A Guide to Field Identification. Illustrated by Arthur Singer. New York, Golden Press, 1966.

ROBERTS, THOMAS S. Bird Portraits in Color. Minneapolis, Univ. of Minn., 1960.

SAUNDERS, ARETAS A. Introduction to Bird Life for Birdwatchers. New York, Dover, 1954.

SCHUTZ, WALTER. Bird Watching, Housing and Feeding. Milwaukee, Wisc., Bruce, 1963.

SMITH, HARRY R., and PARMALEE, PAUL. Distributional Checklist of the Birds of Illinois. Springfield, Ill. State Museum, Popular Science Series No. 4, 1955.

RECORDINGS:

Cornell Laboratory of Ornithology, Ithaca, New York.
Dawn in a Duckblind
An Evening in Sapsucker Woods
American Bird Songs
Music and Bird Songs
Songbirds of America
Birdsongs in Your Garden

National Geographic Society, Washington, D. C.
Song and Garden Birds of North America
(included with book)

Field Guide to the Birds
(Accompanies book of same title by Roger Tory Peterson.)

THE call of the loon is heard among birch woods and across silent lakes in the North Country — a wild, hysterical laughter that gave rise to the story of a mysterious woman who, in search of her lost child, fell shrieking into the dark lake. At that mad cry the moose at the water's edge raises its dripping muzzle from the weeds to listen, and the lone canoeist, pausing in mid-lake, feels a shiver run over him at the wildness of that eerie bird call.

But far away from birch woods and northern lakes one day in spring or autumn, a strange, lone swimmer appears on an Illinois lake, stays for a while far out on deep water, and then is gone. On a winter day the loon is seen once more as it swims and dives on the bright blue waters of the Gulf of Mexico.

The loon is a low-slung bird with a sharp beak and a long neck; the bird sits rather deeply on the water and dives with the suddenness and finality of magic. In autumn plumage the breast and throat are white, the upperparts a smooth, dull, dark grey; in spring, however, the loon comes sharply into focus, a pen-and-ink sketch, clean black and white against the slapping lake water. The black upperparts are thickly speckled with white spots; the underparts are pure white; a black and white band encircles the throat. In this crisp plumage the loon travels northward once more and lays two greenish-brown eggs along the edge of a swampy island. And again that wild shaking laughter, seldom uttered during the long migration journey, rings out across the land of the loon.

The loon is truly a denizen of big water and sky. It is seldom seen more than a few feet away from the water's edge, then only when tending the two large mottled eggs on a reed mat nest but a few inches above the water.

An expert swimmer and diver, the loon captures its food by diving and pursuing it beneath the surface. The loon, like a hydroplane, requires a long running start, skittering and splashing across the surface of the water to gain sufficient speed for the short wings to lift the heavy body in rapid flight.

Illinois Status: Fairly common migrant and uncommon winter resident on Lake Michigan. An uncommon migrant in the rest of the State.

Common Loon
(32 inches)

16

O N the glassy surface of the pond a little, duck-like creature dives and dabbles, a quiet, self-contained swimmer, the pied-billed grebe. To escape danger, or when frightened, the grebe dives, or simply sinks out of sight. Literally changing its specific gravity by forcing air from body sinuses, this bird can sink to any desired level in the water, sometimes only the bill and eyes remaining above water to study a real or fancied danger. Or it may surface dive and stay down in the depths so long that it might almost have drowned, or fallen prey to a turtle. But suddenly, sometimes a long distance from the point where the bird went down, the little head pops up like a submarine periscope and looks around.

The pied-bill, smallest of the grebes, is always known by its small, compact body, which is apparently tailless. The thick beak in spring is marked by a black band, hence the name of "pied" or banded. And even though it may be mistaken for a baby duck, it is only the grebe than can drop, plummet-like, into deep water.

This trick of diving instead of flying is characteristic of the grebes. The pied-bill's wings are used strenuously twice a year on the long migration flights, at other times but seldom.

In early summer in marshy places and in the northern swamps, a nest is built of damp waterweeds and dead cattails—an unsubstantial nest which all but floats away in the marsh. Here the four to eight dull white eggs are laid. Soon after they hatch, the strikingly marked young tumble off the raft and paddle away or ride on their mother's back, perhaps in genuine relief to be gone from their damp bed.

It may be a long way from the marsh to an Illinois park pond, yet on almost any bit of water, large or small, pied-billed grebes may be seen in spring and autumn.

Illinois Status: Common migrant and summer resident in north and central sections. Permanent resident in south but less common in summer.

Pied-billed Grebe
(13½ inches)

18

BEFORE most ducks arrive in autumn, and again in spring, great flocks of dour black cormorants in late afternoon fly in splendid formations up and down the lake, the river, or far inland. Huge, perfect V's, long lines, or echelons, the formations change from one design to another until the sunset goes and the cormorants come down on the water or roost in shore trees for the night. From the weird guttural croakings of drowsy cormorants in their roost-trees in the dark night, one might imagine them prehistoric flying lizards perched on ancient sea cliffs of long ago.

The double-crested cormorant is almost as large as a small goose, in adult plumage is black from head to tail, has a long neck, and four webbed toes that do a good job of swimming or surface diving. When it rests on the water, the cormorant is known from other water birds by the snaky appearance of head and neck. In flight the more nearly equal proportions of tail and neck distinguish it from a flying Canada goose or a black duck for which, in dull weather, it is often mistaken. But the cormorant is far from being a goose. The short legs are set so far back on the body that on shore the bird must sit upright like a penguin. A small orange sac under the beak, proof that this bird is second cousin to a pelican, is sometimes distended with undigested fish when the cormorant, as so often happens, gorges itself on minnows or hickory shad. Then the fierce green eyes grow dull; the bird flies heavily to a tree or to a channel marker in midstream and sits in meditation, like an impatient demon, waiting for the meal to digest and hunger to return.

Sometimes the cormorants sit upright on snags or stumps in river or marsh, spread their wings wide, and sun themselves.

Cormorants pursuing fish are often caught in commercial fish nets, weirs and traps. As a result, many fishermen look on the cormorant at best as a nuisance, at worst as a competitor to be destroyed even though it is protected by both State and Federal laws.

Illinois Status: Fairly common migrant and nester along the Illinois and Mississippi rivers in central section. A fairly common permanent resident but uncommon nester in southern part.

Double-crested Cormorant
(30 inches)

THE great blue heron is like a creature from a wilder environment than Illinois provides — a bird with a seven-foot wingspan and a masterful flight, a lean, wiry bird with a long fish-spear for a beak. The great blue heron (often erroneously called a crane) is an excellent fisherman. All spring and summer and far into the autumn it wades the lakeshores, the river swamps, and marshes in search of fish, frogs, and crayfish. It is a statuesque bird. A quiet pose is needful if fish are not to be frightened away, and so the heron practices something of that admirable Oriental restraint in waiting. In its motionless attitude there is power, action — action held back until the exact moment when it is needed. Then the fish-spear flashes, a small fish is impaled, is twisted around with the head pointed down the long throat, and with a gulp is swallowed.

In the position of watchful waiting, the heron's neck is drawn in, with a great bristly tuft of neck feathers to accent the curve of the throat. The body is delft blue and grey, with a dash of white on crown and throat, especially in the old males. In flight the heron opens its enormous wings and seems to row the air as a boatman rows his boat—powerful, slow wingbeats that show the dark blue or slate-grey portions of the vast pinions; the neck is drawn in, the legs trail. In this all herons differ from cranes and ibises which fly with the neck and legs extended.

Perhaps no bird of the truly wild places is more generally recognized. However, few people ever see the fascinating rookeries where sizeable colonies of these birds rear their young in large stick nests high in big trees, usually in rather isolated mature floodplain forests. Rookeries often exist in the same places for several years. The din of the hoarse calls of adults and young reminds one of a pride of hungry lions growling and snarling over their dinner, and the odor of dead fish and droppings of hundreds of these big fish-eating birds can be very rank on a hot, humid day.

Illinois Status: Fairly common migrant and summer resident throughout the State and a fairly common winter resident in the southern part.

**Great Blue Heron
(46 inches)**

WHITE wings against a summer sky, white bodies that move in a long procession across the sunset and the limpid colors of the marsh — pure white, so snowy that they stand out like unreal creatures against the water and the waving, green acres of cattail, sedge, and weeds. Egrets . . . they come to the midsummer marshes.

When July lowers the water in lake and river and leaves broad expanses of mud flat, large flocks of these splendid southern birds flutter white as paper against the dark mud and lush summer greenery of Illinois. They bring a picture of the far South, a picture painted in the tenuous grey of Spanish moss draped on stunted cypresses in the Everglades; in the intense blues and greens of palmettos and southern sky — in the white crinum lilies, pink spoonbills, and mangrove tangles. Egrets bring a picture of Avery Island in the salt-mine country of Louisiana, where for years they have been protected and where they nest by thousands along the bayous.

Yet once, not too long ago, the sight of an egret was a rare thing to be marvelled at, one which threatened never again to be seen in Illinois. For years plume hunters went into the swamps, ripped the nuptial feathers from the backs of the parent birds, leaving them to die and the young to perish of hunger, blackflies, and snakes. In an appallingly short time the egrets were almost extinct.

Then came legislative protection, and the egrets throve, multiplied, came back. Today when nesting is over and the young are strong, the egrets leave the Louisiana heronries, the cypresses in Tennessee and southern Illinois, and head northward. Rivers, creeks, and lakes suddenly are host to beautiful white birds that pose, motionless, at the water's edge or stand knee-deep in mud and water to wait for a passing fish. These birds have lately extended their breeding range and now nest far up the Illinois and Mississippi rivers. The egret has come back to its ancient homeland.

Illinois Status: Fairly common postbreeding summer visitor throughout the State. Several nesting colonies in south and central and at least one rookery in the north near Rock Island.

Common Egret
(Great Egret)
(41 inches)

24

DURING recent years, three smaller white herons have become increasingly common in Illinois — the little blue heron, the snowy egret, and the cattle egret. As an adult, the little blue heron is slaty-blue; but the immature bird is a snowy-white with only tinges of blue in the wings.

The common egret, although larger, is often confused with the immature little blue heron, for both are white with dark legs and feet. The careful observer, however, will check for the yellow bill of the common egret and the dark bill of the little blue heron.

Still rare in Illinois is the snowy egret which occasionally comes in with the wandering flocks of common egrets in late summer. Like the little blue heron, it too has dark legs and bill, but its feet are bright yellow. This small egret is often referred to as the heron with the "golden slippers."

The third, a newcomer to North America, is the African cattle egret. Sometime in the 1920's or 1930's, a few of these birds crossed the Atlantic (perhaps during a storm) and became established in British Guiana. As the colony increased, some made their way across the Caribbean Islands to South Florida in the 1950's; and now in their wanderings they are spreading north and west. They seem to prefer to feed on the insects stirred up by the feet of cattle. Thus a white heron seen wandering about in a pasture instead of fishing in a marsh is likely to be a cattle egret. It has a somewhat shorter, stockier yellow bill and dark, almost orange-yellow legs. An adult in breeding plummage will have brown patches on its head, breast and back.

The cattle egret, having succeeded in immigrating by its own power, is an interesting addition to the New World species. Its adaptation to the new environment will be fascinating to watch.

Illinois Status: Snowy egret and little blue heron are postbreeding summer visitors throughout the State. A few herons nest along the Mississippi River in the southern part. The cattle egret is beginning to appear in Illinois upland meadows.

top to bottom: Snowy Egret   (24 in.)
Little Blue Heron (immature) (25 in.)
Cattle Egret   (22 in.)

FROM wooded bank or thickety stream an indignant slate-grey and brown bird unfolds from a hunched position of watchful waiting and with a squawk flies up the shore. When it is fishing near the water, the bird seems no larger than a small pullet; but when the wings unfold and that incredible neck stretches forth, when the small greenish crest rises in excitement, the orange legs dangle, and the yellow eyes blaze, then the green heron appears more than twice its apparent size—a gawky, garish surprise in feathers. In flight it is a compact bird — almost the size and shape of a crow — with neck drawn in and short legs almost out of sight.

The green heron is often called "Fly-Up-The-Creek" and "Shite-poke," and is known to more people than perhaps any other heron. It is so common that every pond and creek may have its quota. The slate-bluish wings, the twiddling, stubby tail, and red-brown head and neck and dark green crest are a familiar sight to the fisherman or the hiker, and the harsh cry of "Ske-ow!" hoarsely uttered on the wing is enough to identify the green heron even when the bird itself is out of sight.

These birds come in late March or early April and build a large nest of sticks in a thicket near water, where, in early summer, the four pale bluish-green eggs are laid. Unlike most members of the family, the green heron prefers a solitary location, not a colony, for its nest.

Illinois Status: Common migrant and summer resident throughout the State.

Green Heron
(Green-backed Heron)
(17 inches)
(plant: water-plantain)

OCTOBER — and in the north there is a growing exodus of flying things. Out of the vast Canadian marshes where, for a brief summer, the geese nest and rear their young; out of the tundras where even now water freezes on the ponds at night—out, with a pushing north wind behind them, come the geese heading south.

They were restless long before October. The blue and snow geese, the big Canada geese and their smaller counterparts, the Hutchins's geese, moved away from their midsummer breeding grounds, moulted their worn feathers, and in the marshes and lush grass country fed for weeks before they set out. Then as the first hint of autumn came to the goose country, the flocks gathered together and with the lead-gander at the head, they moved southward.

Sometimes on a night when low-hung clouds send down a cold rain and summer suddenly seems far away, the lights of town reflected on the clouds form an illusion which sometimes confuses the otherwise canny geese. They break ranks, change formations, move circling and calling. Above the lighted business district the moving flocks of honking birds are picked out in silver, like constellations against the night, as they fly about in apparent confusion, until the mysterious compass which guides every goose and gander sends them all to the south again.

There is a strange, nostalgic longing in most people when they see and hear the geese go over in autumn or in spring. It is a longing which yet is somewhat assuaged at sight of those which pass high overhead in a long V, by those which call in the blackness of night, or which come down for a few days on the waters of lake, river, or marsh.

Southern Illinois is a prime winter home of these geese. Ninety per cent of the Canada geese of the Mississippi flyway winter within 100 miles of the confluence of the Ohio and Mississippi rivers. Hundreds of thousands of these great birds winter on the Horseshoe Lake Refuge near Cairo and on the Little Grassy Lake Refuge near Carbondale. Even the giant Canada goose which was thought to be extinct has reappeared in these great winter flocks. It is good to welcome back the great flocks of geese in ever-increasing numbers after the low point in their population in the 1930's.

Illinois Status: Common migrant and abundant winter resident in southern section.

Canada Goose
(39 inches)

THE mallard in all its gleaming beauty is still one of the most abundant of American ducks, the one most sought after in the hunting season. Mallards come by thousands to lakes and marshes; they sit on the water, come on shore to preen their feathers, or gather on a growing edge of ice and at intervals fly out to the cornfields for gleanings left from harvest.

Twilight comes fast in late November — chill, grey twilight, damp with the mists that rise from swamp water. The air is cold; a sharp glaze of ice already has gathered at the waterline among the cattails.

Off across the stillness of the winter marsh the sky is marked with black figures, moving closer, coming into focus as streams of flying things. The sky is full of them. Ducks. Down they come, dash low across the swamp, drop down from the sky, quack and splash into the water. The last gun boomed at four p.m. and now the silence of late autumn is broken only by the splashing of ducks. Out of the sky they come, hundreds of them, thousands of them, unknown quantities of them, shutting out the remaining light with their eager wings. Splendid mallard drakes, green heads glistening, white collars and chestnut fronts picked out in the last glow of sunset, backs a neat brown, orange feet spread wide, and black and white tail feathers fanned out, brake sharply and come down from a height. Night closes down, and the quacking continues, sleepy, occasionally argumentative, in the cold November swamp.

Mallards are the best known of the puddle ducks — so named because they feed in shallow water where they can tip up and reach food on the bottom without diving. Another characteristic of puddle ducks is the bright, metallic wing-patch called a speculum. In the mallard, the speculum is a bright, metallic greenish-blue bordered by bands of black and white. In taking off, puddle ducks seem to explode from the water with a startled leap directly into rapid flight without the running start needed by diving ducks.

Illinois Status: Common migrant and fairly common summer resident locally in central and northern parts. In southern Illinois, a common fall, winter, and spring resident but seldom remains to nest.

**Mallard
(23 inches)**

WHERE shore weeds make shivering reflections in the April lake, a group of ducks floats quietly, resting after the early morning hunt for food. Their colors blend with weeds and water so well that as ducks they are hardly noticeable. White patches in the feather pattern break up the apparent outlines of the bodies so that they become, not ducks, but masses of drift, bits of white foam, or snags jutting from the water.

This is the secret of the ducks, the secret of their concealment in the open. Those patches of light and dark hide them well, and in addition serve as easily remembered marks of identification.

The markings are most brilliant in spring. Then the ducks go north to nest, and in the stress of nesting and caring for the young, the feathers become draggled and worn. As moulting takes place in midsummer, the plummage changes to dull colors, called the "eclipse plumage." This protection just now is very necessary; the wing feathers have been moulted and flight is neither easy nor swift. The ducks must hide. Soon, however, bright new feathers have grown, and on clean, strong, powerful wings the ducks again head south.

Yet even with flight unimpaired, ducks can conceal themselves with those very markings which sometimes seem too bright. The blue-winged teal, a soft, mottled brown with a white crescent on the face, a white mark near the tail, and a large blue patch on the wing, hides in full view. The little green-winged teal, small and shy, has a white mark before and behind, marks that break up its apparent shape and hide it in the open. The big, low-slung shoveler, with its spoon-shaped beak for straining small creatures from the water, is very brightly colored with its white, blue, black, and russet feathers; yet at rest it often seems to melt into its surroundings and is hidden.

Illinois Status: All are fairly common migrants throughout the State. Blue-winged teal is a fairly common nesting species in northern marshes.

upper right.	Shoveler (Northern Shoveler) (also in flight)	(20 in.)
left:	Blue-winged Teal (male below)	(16 in.)
foreground:	Green-winged Teal	(14 in.)

34

MARCH, and the pintails are on the wing. The ice went out of the lake two weeks ago, and from the choppy waters blows a wind that has in it the damp scent of spring, something of the essence of cold water, bare willows, and the good smell of curled, brown willow leaves lying on the shore. It is March, and all day the pintails rise in small detachments from the lake and head north. All day their streamlined bodies, filled with a strange unrest, fly with a whiffling of wings, back and forth, and then north — north over the willows toward the far nesting country. The pintails began even before sunrise; and, as the sun clears the horizon and the mists steam up from the water, the first shafts of orange light strike flying ducks and illuminate their brown heads, silver bodies, and long white necks.

The pintail is always known by its streamlined perfection. The long tail feathers taper to a point, and the rather long neck is marked down the back by a long brown band. Pintails usually go north earlier than the other ducks. Spring, and that insistent wind pushes from behind, urging them to the great breeding areas of Saskatchewan and Hudson Bay, where on the tundras ducks and geese line warm nests with their own soft breast feathers and rear their young in the brief northern summer.

The pintails come to central Illinois rather early in autumn, stay throughout most of the winter, move south when the lakes freeze, and return very early, long before actual spring is here, to await the call to Canada. They gather in small flocks and mingle with the mallards, black ducks, and other dabblers along shore. As the winter draws definitely to a close, the pintails call loudly, wheel about, dash off in small groups, return, quacking, and then, one day they are gone.

Illinois Status: Common migrant throughout the State. A rare summer resident in northern part.

Pintail
(Northern Pintail)
(29 Inches)

W HEN winter winds battle the open lake and most birds hunt shelter, the big floating flocks of scaup ducks bob up and down on the waves, now hidden, now a drifting black raft on the cold, choppy water. Sometimes the ducks dive into the chill depths for small fish and waterweeds or, in a sudden detachment, wheel and circle over the lake.

Scaups come in late autumn, stay until a long hard freeze makes heavy ice, and then return early in spring to the open lake. They are diving ducks that are easily known by the pattern of black and white on the body — black head, neck, and tail, with a pearly, grey-white "saddle" between. Closer at hand the rounded head and rather stubby, bluish beak further identify the scaup, both the greater and the lesser. Neither should be mistaken for the ring-necked duck with its black back, a white pattern on the dark beak, and a bright white crescent-shaped mark on the grey-white sides.

With the scaups and ring-necks there may be the big white canvasbacks with their red-brown heads, sloping foreheads, long beaks, and black fronts. The redhead has the same color pattern as the canvasback but has a rounded head, stubby beak, and grey body.

The diving ducks are birds of deep water where they dive for their food far below the surface. Diving ducks differ from the puddle ducks not only in this habit of diving for food but also in their manner of taking flight. Instead of leaping from the water in full explosive flight, they run and skitter across the water much like a hydroplane, finally gaining enough momentum to take rapid flight.

Illinois Status: All are common migrants. The scaup is abundant and remains common all winter wherever there is open water. The canvasback remains as a common winter resident in the southern part while only a relatively few redheads remain to winter there.

left to right: Redhead   (19 in.)
Ring-necked Duck (16½ in.)
Canvasback   (21 in.)
Lesser Scaup   (16½ in.)
(female, upper right)

38

WHEN November brings its hordes of ducks out of the north and overnight sets swimming flocks on lake and river, there come the small black and white ducks whose shyness and charm make them the more interesting to find. Perhaps it is a compact flock of buffleheads steaming along like a busy little convoy in mid-lake. Their white sides gleam in the late sunshine, and the large white patch on each puffy head stands out as a distinguishing mark to be remembered. With the buffleheads there may be other small ducks which have the crown black and the cheeks white — ruddy ducks. Their bodies are russet-brown, their beaks blue, their tails ridiculously perked-up, wren-like, unique among ducks.

There may be other ducks in the flock, perhaps the fatter, larger goldeneyes, with their immaculate white sides, black backs, and black heads with the distinguishing mark of a white patch between eye and beak. In flight their grey and white wings make a whistling sound which has given the name of "Whistler" to the goldeneye.

But there may be still other ducks, the shyest of them all, the hooded mergansers. They are slender creatures that keep to themselves or dive out of sight after fish in deep water. In flight they are lean and streamlined; at rest they fluff themselves a little as a black and white crest opens out like a silky fan and gives dignity and an almost foreign beauty to the little black and white merganser.

The common merganser and the red-breasted merganser may appear almost like small loons among these diving ducks; and, like the loons, they are great fishermen with long, hooked, pointed bills rather than the flat bills of other ducks.

Illinois Status: All are late migrants and winter residents with the ruddy ducks and hooded mergansers less common in migration and relatively rare as winter residents. Some ruddy ducks remain as summer residents in the northern part.

left, top to bottom: **Common Merganser (25 in.)**
Ruddy Duck (15 in.)
Hooded Merganser (17½ in.)
right, top to bottom: **Bufflehead (female)**
Bufflehead (male) (15 in.)
Common Goldeneye (20 in.)

40

NESTING in small woods or wood lots, the Cooper's hawk is the most common member of this small group of bird hawks called accipiters. With short, rounded wings and long tails, they are admirably suited for the skilled, rapid, erratic flight of a hunter of the forest. They feed on whatever small creatures are most abundant — rodents and small birds. Chicks and chickens were a common prey when it was customary for them to run free in the farmyard. The Cooper's hawk, normally a beneficial and necessary predator in the animal world, can be disastrous to a farmer's small flock of chickens if perchance it has a nest full of small hawks to feed in a nearby orchard.

Except in migration, accipiters are not common in Illinois. Some Cooper's hawks stay to nest in the wooded hill country of southern Illinois; a few nest throughout the State, but they and the little sharp-shinned hawks, as well as the great goshawks, more commonly move north of Illinois to nest. All of them usually capture their food on the ground rather than capturing birds in flight. They are efficient and skillful hunters.

Like all the hawks and owls, they are now wisely protected by law as a valued and important portion of our fauna. In the days when falconry was the sport of kings, the accipiters were the efficient hunters — especially the large goshawk which could take grouse and pheasants for the falconer's table.

Illinois Status: Fairly common migrant and uncommon summer resident in central and northern parts but fairly common permanent resident in southern Illinois.

Cooper's Hawk
(15½ inches)

42

THE buzzard hawks or buteos swing in lazy sweeping circles high in the sky, floating endlessly on rising currents of warm air. With scarcely a perceptible tilt of wing or tail, they bank and turn in marvelous gliding effortless flight.

What are they doing up there so high? Sometimes they are traveling. These migrating hawks face few enemies in the sky; consequently, unlike the small birds, they migrate in broad daylight, often following precise ancestral flyways as they move north and south with the seasons.

Sometimes, especially in midsummer, they may appear to soar in the high cool air for hours — seemingly for the sheer exhilaration of gliding. At other times, they are engaged in the serious business of survival — hunting food for themselves or the young "giants" in their nests.

Skilled flyers with powerful talons and hooked beak, they are wonderfully equipped as a hunting and food-getting machine. Perhaps most remarkable of all are the marvelous eyes, adjusted to see from great height as we would with a pair of good binoculars. As the bird comes in close, its eye lenses, by the application of controlled muscular force, change shape and focal length for precise, clear near-sighted vision.

Unfortunate is the mouse, gopher, rabbit, bird or snake that moves about in an open field when the red-tailed or red-shouldered hawk is hunting on silent soaring wings above. These common hawks are among our most valued controls on the rodent population of the open fields. They are big, powerful birds that require a great deal of food to feed themselves and their young.

The two most common buteos in Illinois in summer are the red-tailed hawk, illustrated here with plain solid-colored tail with the dark border and the dark, often indistinct, band across the breast, and the red-shouldered hawk with a plain breast but a prominently-banded tail of four or five wide dark bands separated by narrow white bands.

Illinois Status: Fairly common permanent resident throughout the State, less common in the south in summer. Very common migrant throughout the State.

Red-tailed Hawk
(20-23 inches)

44

THE marsh hawk is a big moth-like grey bird that alternately beats and sails on floppy wings over field, marsh, and grassy uplands. It flies so low that the big wings almost touch the ground, and in a business-like manner it efficiently quarters a field, flies up and down in search of mice, snakes, or large insects, and then moves on to another area. In their food preferences, marsh hawks do an uncalculated amount of good in devouring quantities of the small vermin which harm grain.

The marsh hawk is an exceedingly graceful bird that balances and tips on crosscurrents and springtime winds. The male is grey above and pure white below, with a long tail and long wings which have black tips. The female is brown, a trifle larger than the male. Both birds have that characteristic large white patch on the rump. By this mark, and by the peculiar floppy flight, the marsh hawk is easily identified a long distance away.

A bird of open fields, the marsh hawk is the only ground-nesting hawk in Illinois, having a preference for grassy meadows near marshy water. One of the few birds of prey where the sexes are easily distinguished, it is also one of the few where there is a very definite division of responsibilities. The big, brown females tend the nest and the young. The smaller grey males provide most of the food, but they are not permitted at the nest. When the male comes flying in with a newly-captured morsel for his mate or young, he gives a loud excited whistle. The female responds and flies up to meet him. When she comes to a position just a few feet beneath him, she gives a whistle-like scream, banks up toward him, and he drops the food, calling excitedly. She, almost upside down, catches the falling food, rights herself, and takes the food to the nest. There, holding it in her talons, she tears off small dainty bits, eating some herself and feeding the rest to her young ones. This spectacular food exchange takes place several times early each morning and a few times each evening before dusk.

Illinois Status: Common migrant and summer resident in central and northern parts and a common migrant and winter resident in southern part.

**Marsh Hawk
(Northern Harrier)
(19 Inches)**

IN Illinois, the Mississippi and Illinois rivers support one of the few large winter populations of these wonderfully spectacular eagles in North America.

In recent years more than a hundred of these huge birds feed at the water pools below the navigation dams where the tumbling water stays open even in the coldest weather. Here, in the winter, unbelievable concentrations of fish seek the open, aerated water, and the eagles gather, attracted by the abundant food supply.

The bald eagle is readily recognized in flight. It has a massive silhouette with long, blunt wings. The tremendous wingspread is almost twice the bird's length; when soaring, the wings are carried flat and level with the body and the tail is spread like the buteos. Of course, the great white head and tail will identify the adult bird; but for their first three years, the young birds have dark heads and tails.

A scream in the sky, a splash in the lake, and an eruption of splashing, shaking wings brings the osprey, our smallest eagle, out of the water with a wriggling fish grasped in its firm talons. With surprising dexterity, the captured fish is skillfully manipulated to be carried head first in its most streamlined position as the strikingly-marked osprey flies off to a high perch, usually a tall dead branch in the treetops.

Rarely nesting in Illinois, this little eagle is usually seen during spring and fall migration. Like the bald eagle, it has the long wings and short fantail but, in flight, it usually flies on bent wings forming a W-shaped silhouette.

Illinois Status: The bald eagle is a fairly common migrant and winter resident along the Illinois and Mississippi rivers. Uncommon elsewhere. There are a few pairs of resident eagles along the Mississippi in southern Illinois. The osprey is a fairly common migrant along the Illinois and Mississippi river valleys. Uncommon elsewhere. An uncommon local resident in the southern part.

Bald Eagle (35 in.)
Osprey (23 in.)

THE fastest, most spectacular flyers are the falcons — trained since medieval times for the sport of kings and honored by the Hopewellian Indians of Illinois in beautifully designed and faithfully reproduced stone pipes. The smallest of our North American falcons is the sparrow hawk — the only one commonly seen in Illinois.

The sparrow hawk chooses a fence post, a telephone pole, or a dead tree where the view is clear, and perches there for a long time until it sees something moving on the ground — perhaps a grasshopper, perhaps a fat meadow mouse, perhaps a small toad from the spring pond. Instantly the sparrow hawk dashes out from its point of vantage, hovers a minute on beating wings, and drops. It is up again and away, flying back to its perch to dine.

Among the hawks which spend all or part of their time in central Illinois, the little sparrow hawk is commonest and most easily seen along every highway and country lane. The coloring is sharp and distinct; it is a bright red-brown on back and tail, slate-blue on crown and wings, a dark band across the end of the tail; the breast is spotted, and a crisp black mustache-mark curves on each cheek. When the bird is at rest, the tail pumps up and down; when on the wing, the long tail and long sharp wings, and that unique habit of hovering, distinguish it from the other hawks.

The nest is made in an old woodpecker or owl hole in a tree. Both parent birds take turns at feeding the perpetual hunger of the young, which one day come forth to sit in a stub-tailed row on the fence.

Sparrow hawks often come into town where sparrows or starlings are abundant. A few years ago a sparrow hawk that made regular visits into the business district of a large town became the object of intense interest in newspaper columns, offices, and among passersby. Each day at five o'clock the hawk flew into a certain street, snipped a sparrow off an eave, and flew to the top of the city hall to feed.

Illinois Status: A common permanent resident throughout the State.

**Sparrow Hawk
(American Kestrel)
(9½-11 inches)**

THE bobwhite fits into the Illinois scene. The pleasant, cheerful voice becomes a part of country lanes scented with ripe apples and that other ripeness of October leaves, a part of the stubble fields and the shocks of corn stacked yellow against a cobalt sky. The running birds leap into the air and glide on bowed wings into the grass; the bobwhite whistles, and the countryside acquires new satisfaction.

When winter comes, the bobwhites maintain their family flocks and all day hunt seeds in the weed patches. As the cold light of winter sunset draws near and the purple shadows grow on the snowbanks, the plaintive whistle of the bobwhite calls the flock together for the night. They gather beneath a bush, sit in a compact circle, tails together, heads out, for warmth and for protection. At the sound of danger they burst in all directions into the air and vanish into the weeds.

Spring — and again the voice of the bobwhite calls throatily from a fence post. Soon there are a dozen white eggs laid in a nest placed in a tangle of grass or in the shelter of a fence corner. Soon the young bobwhites, fluffy and babyish, go trotting along after their mother who keeps a constantly watchful eye for snakes, hawks, and weasels, and at the slightest hint of danger, clucks warningly. Instantly the babies vanish in their tracks, hide somehow in the open, until a reassuring call brings them to their feet again. The bobwhite family has a call for every need and mood; and perhaps it is not more lovely than on a warm summer day when bobwhites whistle among the waving wheat.

Of all the native upland game birds of Illinois, the bobwhite alone has adapted to the farm fields and woodlots of Illinois' modern agriculture. The ruffed grouse and the sharp-tailed grouse are gone. The prairie chicken is hanging on with only a tiny remnant. The wild turkey has also disappeared but is now being reintroduced in southern Illinois.

Illinois Status: Permanent resident throughout the State but uncommon to rare in the northern part.

Bobwhite
(Northern Bobwhite)
(10 inches)
(plant: wheat)

A MAGNIFICENT gamecock, strutting lord of thicket and upland pasture, a brilliant creature slipping into immediate concealment — that's the ring-necked pheasant. It is like something escaped from game farm or zoo, yet the pheasant today is as wild and wary as any grouse or prairie chicken.

A long time ago, however, the pheasant was a cultivated bird; it was introduced by the Romans into Europe from the region of the River Phasis in Colchis. The bird was interbred with Chinese pheasants to produce the present ring-necked form, later was brought to America and released for naturalizing. The pheasant has taken full advantage of its freedom: It has multiplied and spread throughout most of the country until in some places it has become very common. Yet all the while it is as wild as any native bird — wild, with the wariness which sends it bursting into the air, wings whirring, plumes trailing, and every brilliant feather agleam.

The male is an elegant creature with a long, golden-brown tail, the trophy of many a pheasant hunt. The purple and green head has two slight crests, or ears. There is a patch of red skin on the face, a white collar around the neck, a bright russet-red breast, and short, rounded, brown wings that move in a whirring rush. The female is a dull, mottled, brown bird with a shorter tail, a meek little hen that creeps unobtrusively to the nest hidden in long grass, while the pompous cock struts for all the world to see and then goes slinking off, brilliance strangely hidden, along the weedy fencerow.

Every effort has been made to introduce the pheasant as an effective game bird throughout the State, but to date only in certain areas in the northern third of Illinois has its residence been successfully established.

Why so few are found south of the Bloomington-Champaign area is an unsolved mystery. Almost every year sportsmen, scientists and conservationists propose and try some new attack on the problem. However, satisfactory and workable solutions to this problem of adaptation and distribution are still unknown.

Illinois Status: A common permanent resident in the northern part and in the Grand Prairie of the east-central section. Uncommon to rare in the rest of the State.

Ring-necked Pheasant
(30 inches)

PERHAPS the wilderness areas in Illinois least disturbed by man are the marshlands scattered along the river channels throughout the length and breadth of the State and among the terrestrial moraines of northern Illinois. Cattail and sedge marshes are difficult of access and harbor many of the same creatures that have filled these ecological niches for eons. It is little wonder that some of the least known and the most fascinating birds of our entire bird population live out their lives seldom seen by man though often in close proximity to him.

The tangled debris in the small clogged waterways is teeming with life especially adapted to it. The strange calls and sounds that emerge from these marshes are often a discordant mixture of sounds emitted by insects, amphibians, and a surprising number of birds. The rails are among the most interesting of any of the birds found there. These short-winged, weak flying birds are poor swimmers. They have extremely long toes which support them well on the floating debris, and they run agilely where other creatures sink. Hidden from view in the tangled mass, the rails are uniquely adapted to life in this strange and primitive habitat.

The king rail, almost pullet-sized and with a long dark beak, is the largest Illinois member of this family. It utters loud startling grunts with great rapidity which, on a spring night, roll across the bog and die away.

More common than the king rail is the smaller sora rail with its little yellow beak and its harsh, descending, derisive "laugh." Or, as Virginia Eifert more pleasingly described it: "Its eerie whinny wakes the marsh when dawn lays paint-color in the still pools between the cattails."

The Virginia rail is a small dark edition of the king rail. It, too, has a long dark beak, the barred sides and stubby tail.

The young of the rails are also of great interest — tiny chicks, all black, that run about among the reeds at the water's edge under the observant eye of the adult.

To become acquainted with these interesting birds in this special niche, stop beside a marsh, sit in the car or stand quietly, and watch the open edges of the water, the places where opportunity affords a glimpse into the ground level of the marsh. In a period of time, surely you will spot some rails moving busily about with no thought or concern of an outside world.

Illinois Status: Fairly common migrant and summer resident where there is suitable habitat. The Virginia and sora rails are more common in the northern marshes than elsewhere in the State.

King Rail and young
(15 inches)

THE coot exemplifies a remarkable adaptation to a slightly different niche. Closely related to the rails, the coot has long toes which allow it to walk on reeds and sedge mats; yet its toes, unlike those of the rail, are lobed with paddles, making it also an excellent swimmer in the open water.

Often derisively referred to as "ridiculous," "incautious," and called "mud hen" and "fool hen," coots nevertheless have survived in larger numbers and more successfully than most of the waterfowl. Because they so often move about in little groups in the open water near the shore, they are commonly known to almost every sportsman or casual observer of the out-of-doors.

Dark slate-grey in color, these little birds look black against the water, their bright white bills and white undertail coverlets appearing as headlights and taillights as they move along.

Although these birds have always been included on the waterfowl hunting lists and larger possession limits have been allowed than for other waterfowl, they nevertheless survive, perhaps because they are unpopular with both the hunter and the cook. Their food consists of varieties of little aquatic creatures living in the mud flats and in the shallow waters, and these impart to the flesh a strong fishy odor, palatable only to a limited number of sportsmen. Coupled with this is the fact that they are so foolhardy and bold that they hardly afford a good target to challenge the sportsman's pride. These factors may have helped make the coot more abundant when other waterfowl were becoming scarce.

Coots are weak flyers, wings apparently small in comparison to body weight, and they must aquaplane along on the water, running and flying, for long distances before they gain sufficient speed to become airborne.

Illinois Status: Found commonly in open water, during spring and fall migrations. Many remain in winter as long as the water remains open. A few nest locally in central and northeastern Illinois.

American Coot
(15 inches)
(plant: wild iris)

THE killdeer is one of the few Illinois birds that resorts to a trick in leading danger away from the eggs or young. A passing dog, a human being, an automobile, or a grazing horse may be treated to the sight of what appears to be a mortally wounded bird flopping and kicking on the ground. All the while, a canny bright eye is kept on all the onlooker's movements as slowly the bird leads danger away from the nest. At a safe distance and with a derisive "kill-dee!" the bird takes wing and flies off as well as ever. It is an old killdeer trick, one which has probably saved many a killdeer nest and eggs from almost certain destruction.

Nests of killdeers are found in the most unlikely places. Four large cone-shaped, pebble-colored eggs are laid almost in the open. In the middle of a shale road, a stony field, the furrow of a newly plowed cornfield, on golf courses, in pastures and airports, these birds incubate their eggs and raise their precocious young. When the eggs hatch, the well-developed young killdeers are ready to run and to feed.

Instinctively they seem to know the signals which mean danger or safety. The skittering, long-legged, conspicuous little chicks will freeze on the alarm note of their parents and squeeze quietly down against the ground, covering their white breast feathers. Their mottled backs seem to disappear before one's very eyes. The chicks apparently will not move until the parent birds, having led danger away, return and, with another note, release them from their frozen invisibility.

In summer the mud flats are noisy with the petulant voices of the killdeers, but it is in late winter that the voice of the killdeer means most to those who are hungry for a sign of spring. Out of the chill March sky comes flying a silver-winged bird whose voice means spring to the world below. Sometimes at night, when the moon is misty, and the spring stars gleam softly, the mysterious voices of killdeers come from somewhere in the night — calling, calling, to make springtime a reality.

Illinois Status: Common permanent resident in the southern part and a common migrant and summer resident in central and northern parts.

Killdeer
(10½ inches)

THE whirring rhythmic music of "feather songs" above a
marshy willow brake is perhaps the most exciting sound of
spring to even the most sophisticated bird observer. The woodcock,
a strange denizen of the bird world that looks as unreal in life as
it does in pictures, fills a unique and specialized niche.

Even smaller than the quail, this little bird is so well camou-
flaged that an observer may come quite close and not see it until
an explosive and erratic burst of flight reveals its presence. Its
eyes, placed far back on the head, give vision in all directions even
while the bird is busily probing its long bill full-length into the
soft mud in search of food. The bill is so uniquely adapted that
when a grub or worm is found, the front part can be opened to
grasp it and pull it from the ground.

Early spring is the best time to see the woodcock. In April at
sundown, when twilight is laying its last colors on the water, the
vocal call of the woodcock will come from the willow brakes — a
strident, harsh, beep-like call reminding one of the call of the
night hawk. If the observer is stationed at the edge of the forest
opening where he can observe the darkening sky, he may soon
see rising from the thicket in an ascending circular spiral the
male woodcock as he climbs into the evening sky. Then the nuptial
flight of the woodcock begins. The sound apparently produced by
the wind against the four thinly-webbed, outer primary wing
feathers of the bird is a strange, winnowing, whirring, rhythmic
sound, like a switch whisked back and forth — the spring song of
the bog sprite — and after a few moments, as suddenly as it
started, the "feather song" will stop. If the observer watches the
sky closely, he will suddenly see a little ball drop from the sky,
plummeting to the ground close to where the bird first leaped
into the air to start this nuptial flight. After a few minutes, the
performance will begin again — an exciting and unbelieveable
exhibition which lends drama to the mood of the evening sky.

Illinois Status: A rare summer and winter resident in the southern part. A
somewhat irregular migrant and uncommon resident in the rest of the State.

American Woodcock
(11 inches)

SOMETIMES at night or on a lovely day in spring, a weird, eerie call comes from somewhere in the upper sky — a long, drawn-out whinny that is almost like the voice of the wind. The whinny heralds the approach of a lean, sharp-winged bird that comes flying out of the sky, utters again that strange call as it drops down to a post, raises long wings high, claps them briskly against its sides, and stands in wide-eyed contemplation of the highway. This is the Flying Horse, or upland plover. The cry and the characteristic manner in which the bird, on alighting, raises Pegasean wings give basis to the name.

This plover is a long-legged, long-necked, light brown creature which often becomes one of the first birds to excite a potential birdlover's interest. It is a puzzle to many a motorist who passes along the highway and sees that strange, lank-legged, sandpiper standing on telephone post or fence.

The upland plover is often called Bartramian sandpiper and has all the characteristics of a shore-bird and a wader, certainly not those of a perching bird. Yet when it walks with a sneaking sort of gait through pasture grass and upland stubble, it may not even be recognizable as the same bird that stood on a post.

The plover is fondest of sunny, dry uplands and summer pastures; there in June the nest is built and the four or five creamy-buff, speckled eggs are laid.

This bird, abundant in the early days of the upland prairie, was almost eliminated from the American scene by indiscriminate shooting and the destruction of the prairie. In the 1920's and 1930's it was thought to be gone from most of the range, and there was little hope that the species would survive. But the halt to indiscriminate shooting in the middle 1930's and the ability of the bird to adapt to golf courses, airports and pasture lands has brought its return, not in the former abundance, but in sufficient numbers so that any careful bird observer can find them scattered over the prairie regions of America.

Illinois Status: Fairly common migrant and summer resident locally in suitable grassland nesting habitat. Appears to be increasing in abundance, especially in the central and southern sections.

Upland Plover
(Upland Sandpiper)
(11½ inches)
(plant: blackberry)

O N the shores of the park pond — upon the thick, dank mud of the riverbank, or on the mud flats and sandbars of any water-course in Illinois—there runs a teetering, tipping little sandpiper. Among all the sandpipers—a large tribe notoriously difficult to identify—the little spotted sandpiper stands out distinctly, a freckled gamin among the meeker markings of its brethren. The spotted sandpiper goes tottering and tilting along with what appears to be an enormous amount of wasted energy. Its whole body tilts with the simplest stride; and when the bird is disturbed or merely curious, it seems that the little, unsteady body will become unhinged from the spindly legs.

The spotted sandpiper has spots — and that's the best way to identify it, because no other sandpiper has such distinct and abundant markings on the undersides. The bird flies with a "twittering" flight which turns into a bowed glide. In flight the bird is identified by the double white line along the middle of the wing.

A great many other sandpipers come to the mud flats and spillways in late summer. The solitary sandpiper, somewhat larger than the spotted, is a smooth, darker brown above with a wash of grey on the throat and breast, white underparts, dark legs, and a white ring around the eye. In flight a black band is visible down the middle of the white, lightly barred tail.

The fall plumage of the spotted sandpiper is not so easily identified when the spots have given way to a plain white breast and the russet tone of the back appears quite grey. Then it is the teetering habit and distinctive two-note call which alerts one to its presence. A disinctive white shoulder patch will further aid in identifying this common shore-bird.

Illinois Status: Common migrant throughout the State and a common summer resident in the central and northern part, but only rarely remains as a nesting species in the southern section.

Spotted Sandpiper
(7½ inches)
(plant: arrowhead)

SOMETIMES in spring and again in August, the wet mud flats of river, lake or prairie pond will offer more tantalizing birds per square foot than perhaps any other Illinois environment. The wet mud is crisscrossed with small three-toed footprints of sandpipers, plovers and snipe. There may be as many as seventeen common varieties of these shore-birds and sometimes some five to seven rarer species, all feeding with complete concentration in a very small area of exposed wet mud and shallow water, usually only two or three inches deep.

These birds are a most difficult group to learn, literally the postgraduate course in field identification. As a group they are neat and trim, predominantly grey and white, and many have distinctive voices, movements and flight patterns which are helpful in identification.

Two which stand out are the yellowlegs, the greater and lesser. They are chiefly known by the thin, straight, yellow shanks which stand out brightly in contrast to the darker legs of most other waders. The yellowlegs is grey above, light grey and white below. There is a slight eye-ring. In flight the yellowlegs is a dark-winged shore-bird with a conspicuous white rump and tail. The greater yellowlegs has a slightly upturned beak; the lesser has a straight bill.

Pictured on the opposite page with the lesser yellowlegs are two least sandpipers. They are streaked brown on back and wings, and lightly streaked brown on grey-white breasts — tiny, intent, round-shouldered waders busily exploring the shores.

The trim little bird with the large head and short blunt bill of the plovers is the semipalmated plover. It appears like a diminutive killdeer with but one black collar band. It is one of the more striking and easily identified shore-birds.

Illinois Status: All are more or less common migrants through Illinois.

top:	Lesser Yellowlegs	(10½ in.)
bottom left:	Semipalmated Plover	(6¾ in.)
bottom right:	Least Sandpipers	(6 in.)

WHITE GULLS soar and dip over the lake, scream from the ice, swoop into a blue sky. Gulls — magnificent birds bred on ocean shores — are wild, free, full of speed and grace, with that cynical invincibility which, with a laugh and a swirl of white wings, mocks danger and the elements.

When autumn comes, the first of the large herring gulls and the smaller, more abundant ring-bills appear on the watercourses of central Illinois. The gulls increase in numbers until ice covers the entire water and the supply of fish is cut off. Only then do they move farther south, sometimes as far as the Gulf of Mexico; but as soon as the ice rips and thunders under a warming sun, the birds return. In March they are very abundant, especially along the shores where wind and wave bring in dead fish and debris. With wild, eerie, resounding calls, the gulls swoop and almost submerge for fish, or sit like queer, white, high-tailed ducks on the water.

These large mature gulls with snow-white heads, breasts, and tails are bright against the sky as they dip and bank, showing their blue-gray wings tipped with black. The dull immature plumages of the bulky young are in sharp contrast to the glossy adults, the young herring gulls in tones of brown, the ring-bills in tones of gray.

Gulls are one of the few creatures in our world that can live in both freshwater and saltwater environments—being able to eliminate the excess salt through a special salt gland near the eye.

Gulls are predators and scavengers, swooping excitedly and noisely for chunks of bread or dead fish, gorging themselves at a garbage dump, raiding a bird colony for young birds and eggs, or cleaning up insects behind a farmer's plow or waste material behind a fisherman's boat. Wherever one gull discovers food, quickly a flock gathers stealing from one another with noisy but always graceful abandon.

Illinois Status: Both are common migrants. Some non-breeding birds remain as summer residents. Some gulls remain all winter wherever there is open water, herring gulls predominantly on the big water of Lake Michigan and the Mississippi and Ohio rivers, ring-bills predominantly on smaller inland lakes.

Ring-billed Gull
(18 inches)

THEY are the spirit of the salt wind and the timelessness of the sea. They are the soul of the tide-beach and the driftwood, part of the dunes, the waving sea-wheat, and the unending noise of the ocean. Terns are the sea, and the sea would be empty without them.

Far out over the water flash powerful white wings. Like efficient ships' sails, they carry slim bodies in bounding, swallow-like flight. Up and down the shore they fly, regularly, as if they knew a predetermined track. A sea-chantey cackle, a dip, a dive, an upward swirl of swallowtail and long white wings—these are the terns, wild and as free as the ocean, as much a part of the beach scene and the barnacle-grown wharf as the salt smell and the surf.

Something of this feeling of ocean comes to Illinois when the terns visit the lakes in spring and summer. Next to seeing the ocean itself there is the thrill of seeing terns — common terns, Forster's terns, the big Caspians, and occasionally the tiny least tern, all of them salty mariners on shore leave. Most of them, with individual variations, have that characteristic marking — black cap, beak pointed downward, forked tail, white body. One tern, however, differs. Every spring and summer the black terns, natives of inland swamps, come in unified flocks to fly up and down the lakes and fields in search of insects; often they fly over water and dip down for a small fish. These birds have grey wings and black bodies, with a dash of white and that same crisp, nautical wingbeat that belongs to terns and oceans, no matter how far inland the birds may be. Black terns or white, they are exciting and wild — wild and free as the waters which they love.

Illinois Status: Black tern is common migrant in central and northern parts. Summer resident in north. Common tern is common migrant.

left: **Black Tern** (10 in.)
right: **Common Tern** (15 in.)

FROM pines in the cemeteries, from oaks in the parks, from woods and fencerows and farms in spring, there comes the plaintive cooing of the mourning dove. A heartbroken moan is the dove's expression of happiness; a sigh is its song. The human interpretation of the quality of that song turns it into a dirge.

Out of all the doves in the world, only this species is native to Illinois. Flocks arrive early in March, and the doves begin to nest in April. In a frail handful of twigs set in a thorn tree, an apple tree, a hemlock, or sometimes in a low bush, the dove somehow balances two clean white eggs and broods them until the young hatch. To maintain any sort of protection from falling overboard or through the floor, the young doves cling with their pink feet to the bottom of the nest. For days the dove is pleasantly maternal; she feeds them, watches them as they take their first flight, and then, when they are able to fend for themselves, builds another nest just like the first and starts all over again. This process continues until October, when the hunting season often finds a late batch of young or eggs still in the nest.

The nest is fragile and unbelievably crude, and the young are among the most undeveloped and helpless of any of the young birds. The adults actually pre-digest the food and then secrete a nutritive fluid called pigeon milk which they feed to the young.

The mourning dove has many characteristics of the extinct passenger pigeon; the latter, however, was larger, had more iridescence on the sleek head and back, and had a longer tail. The flight of wild pigeons was silent; dove flight is announced by a loud whistling of wings. Yet the mourning dove has something of that same sleek outline, that slender grace of the wild pigeon, and a long tail which, on alighting, spreads to a brown and white fan, or in flight is streamlined. The dove, unlike the passenger pigeon, travels alone or in pairs, and consequently is not subject to the danger of mass extinction of a large flock.

Illinois Status: Common migrant and summer resident throughout the State and a common permanent resident in the southern part. A few remain through the winter in the rest of the State.

Mourning Dove
(12 inches)
(tree: Scotch pine)

O N a sultry day when the air is too still and there is a feeling of rain somewhere, a hoarse croaking comes from the trees. "There's a rain crow," folks say. "It's calling rain."

The rain crow is the cuckoo, a bird which is fond of tent caterpillars and which eats them in such abundance that if there were only a few more cuckoos in the world, there might be no more caterpillars. The cuckoo has a tough gullet, and a stomach which tolerates fierce caterpillar bristles until the lining is thickly furred with them.

Two cuckoos are found in Illinois, the yellow-billed and the black-billed. Elusive but not uncommon, these large, long-tailed birds are often heard but seldom seen as they move through the heavy foliage of trees and shrubbery. A slim, sinuous form and a stealthy manner are characteristic of all cuckoos.

The yellow-billed cuckoo is a sleek brown bird with rusty shoulders, a white front, and a long tail marked boldly beneath with black and white spots. The beak is dark brown above and yellow below.

The black-billed cuckoo is smaller, greyer, and has an entirely black beak. The habits of the two are similar except that the yellow-billed seems to prefer groves of mature trees while the black-billed is more often found in rather open brushy thickets.

The cuckoo when it alights in a tree turns its head from side to side in a strangely reptilian, almost stupid manner, and then sidles among the leaves where it is immediately hidden. Cuckoos nest in low bushes or trees, and in a nest of twigs like a dove's nest lay two to five pale greenish-blue eggs. These birds arrive in May and depart for the South in September; in this interval they spend their time in ridding caterpillar-infested walnut and hickory trees of devouring pests.

Illinois Status: Yellow-billed is common summer resident throughout the State. Black-billed is a common migrant throughout but a rare summer resident in the southern part and a fairly common resident in the north and central parts.

Yellow-billed Cuckoo
(12¼ inches)
(tree: basswood)

76

IT is autumn, and night has a tinge of chill, a scent of ripened leaves, a premonition, somehow, of winter. The crickety noises of summer have been silenced by frost; high in the darkness there is the faint, far-away twitter of a bird speeding south.

It is autumn — November is near — and a little owl utters a quavering, bubbling call that swells upward from the breath of a wind, and dies in the engulfing silence of autumn. It is almost a human call — the voice of the screech owl.

In autumn the screech owl's call usually is one tone that wavers throatily but in other seasons it ripples up and down the scale, yet often ends on that plaintive autumn note. It is scarcely ever a screech.

Of all the owls of Illinois, the screech owl is the only one which often chooses to live close to man. It is a common owl of cities and suburbs, of lake residential areas and of farmyards. The shrubbery and foliage give shelter, and the small birds and rodents that thrive so abundantly in man's habitat provide an ample food supply. Any tree hollow or large nesting box with about a three-inch opening will shelter both the bird and its nest.

The food consumption of a pair of screech owls with a sizable litter of young is unbelievably large and varied — grasshoppers, beetles, small birds, rodents and reptiles. Whatever is moving about from dusk to dawn will be quickly caught, killed and swallowed whole or fed to the young.

This is the smallest common owl of our area, the only little owl with feather tufts, often called horns. It appears in two color phases, a rich reddish-brown and a soft grey.

Illinois Status: Common permanent resident throughout the State.

Screech Owl
(Eastern Screech Owl)
(9 inches)
(tree: red oak)

"I HEAR an owl speak, and I would rather hear him than the most eloquent man of the age," said Thoreau many years ago. And today other folk may also find a kindred thrill in the mellow, throaty, wild hooting — an eight-hoot call — of the barred owl. It is heard at night, in daylight, and in rain; it is haunting and far-reaching. The owl is still one of the untamables, part of a wilderness as yet unconquered, akin to the rattlesnake, the coyote, and the eagle. It is different from other birds.

Of all members of this elusive, mysterious tribe, the barred owl is perhaps most easily startled out of daydreaming. All day long the big owl sits in a crotch of a tree in the river bottomlands and keeps a wary ear open for noises. When, with a crackling of leaves underfoot, the hunter or hiker comes past, the owl is immediately disturbed, takes wing, and flies to another tree. The big brown wings are silent; a shadow passes through the trees and stops somewhere farther on. A tall, brown, barred bird with no horns on the round head sits upright on a branch, peers with singularly liquid, dark eyes full of curiosity at the approaching hiker, and then flies on again, or doubles back to its bed tree. The dark eyes at once identify the barred owl. Most owl eyes are yellow.

The barred owl may be found in almost any piece of woodland, in parks, and in cemeteries, where there is ample protection in tall trees. Here a pair of owls may take up residence and live for many years, often unknown to the very people who live nearest the region.

Among the seven kinds of owls that commonly live in Illinois, only the two largest ones — the dark-eyed, round-faced barred owl and the yellow-eyed, ear-tufted great horned owl — have a hooting call, the voice traditionally associated with owls.

Illinois Status: The barred owl is common in the river bottom areas and a fairly common permanent resident in all mature wooded areas of the State.

Barred Owl
(20 inches)
(tree: white elm)

THE short-eared owl is an elusive hunter of the grassland prairies — a valued destroyer of rodents that thrive with the development of grain farming. At dusk you may chance to catch a glimpse of the long, slender body and wing silhouette against the sky as you drive along a country road.

To most birds an automobile is not a thing to be feared. Thus the birdlover may often see more of the wilder birds by staying inside his car and driving in as close as possible to the haunts of birds, than by hiking after them. The short-eared owl, which frequents roadsides and fields along the highways, is one of the easiest birds to see in this manner.

On a day in late winter, when a damp chill shut down as sunset sent a deceptively warm yellow light over the bareness of winter wheat and tattered corn, three owls went flying about — day-flying owls, in itself somewhat unusual in a nocturnal family. The golden-brown and white wings seemed very long for the slim bodies and small, round, owl-heads, and flapped with a silent, nighthawk-like flight, effortlessly over the fields, in an endless search for mice.

An owl came down on a fence post and faced the road. Faced it, yes, if one could call it *facing* when the round head went whisking back and forth as if on a well-greased pivot, keeping a sharp eye out in all directions.

A car stopped close by and the occupants watched in fascination as the glistening, gold-rimmed brown eyes darted here and there, yet never, it seemed, in the direction of the car.

Owl's eyes are wonderfully adapted for both day and night vision. The pupils quickly dilate to extremely large size to let in all available light for night vision or close to small pinhead-sized openings to regulate the proper light absorption for daytime. However, the eyes cannot move to look from side to side but are fixed to stare only straight ahead. Therefore, the owl must turn its head to look about.

Illinois Status: Irregular migrant in south. Uncommon permanent resident in central and north.

Short-eared Owl
(13½ inches)

THE nighthawk is not a hawk at all but a relative of the swift and the whip-poor-will. Its tiny bill opens to a large gaping mouth that scoops up the insects in midair.

Once the nighthawk lived solely in the uplands, hunted for insects in the sky and over water, and laid two mottled grey eggs on a barren spot of sun-baked ground. Nighthawks hunted in late afternoon and evening, and during the day they slept on a horizontal limb of a tree, or rested on the ground.

Now the nighthawk has become metropolitan. It still hunts for insects in the sky, but it flies above and between tall buildings, and lays its eggs on the flat roofs. It is commonly attracted to the hordes of insects that gather about brightly-lit theater marquees and used-car lots. Many city nighthawks have even mastered the difficult feat of resting lengthwise on a telephone wire.

The nighthawk is one of the few "backyard birds" which visits alike the sky above country gardens and tenement streets, one of the few common birds big cities know. In summer it is out in all sorts of weather. It exults in a storm. In the midst of thunder and lightning, and in rain that would beat down most birds, the rousing shouts of the nighthawk defy fate and the elements. A great flash of lightning often shows the birds darting crazily back and forth against low-hung clouds.

It is a curious sound, the booming squawk of the nighthawk, and distinguishes the bird when it is too far away to be otherwise identified.

The white "windows" in the nighthawk's long swallow-like wings will readily identify it. At times the bird seems to delight in spectacular tumbling dives, falling for hundreds of feet in uncontrolled free falls. Then as they approach the teeming traffic of a city street, literally tumbling between tall buildings, they spread their wings and tail and take command of their flight with a noisy boom, so loud it can often be heard above the noise of city traffic. As the air currents again catch the lifted surfaces of their wings, they shoot skyward, completing a fantastic aerial maneuver.

Illinois Status: A common migrant and summer resident.

Common Nighthawk
(10 inches)

84

A WHIRRING in the chimney, a weird, high, twittering somewhere above, sickle-winged birds cutting keen parabolas against the sky — what are they, those chimney devils, those skywitches, that inhabit the summer chimneys?

Long before there were people or chimneys in America, the little grey chimney swifts nested in hollow trees and in the dark recesses of caves. With the coming of civilization, however, the swifts were among the first birds to adapt themselves to changing times. They left their caves and tree-hollows and came eagerly into towns; they built frail nests inside the sooty chimneys and went soaring after insects in the air.

The nests are made of short twigs snipped from dead branches and gathered on the wing. In the chimney the twigs are plastered in place with saliva from the birds' capacious mouths. Three or four white eggs are laid in these dangerously-hung nests, and the young soon learn how to cling with their hooked claws, spiny tails, and knobby calloused "elbows" to the rough walls of the chimney.

Sharp, wire-like spines on the tail feathers enable the birds to roost upright in this black hollow; but they cannot perch, they cannot walk, they do not sing, nor do they usually bathe, except in a shower of rain. The feet of swifts, possibly through long centuries of disuse, are good only for clinging, but in flight they live up to their reputation as the speediest birds on earth. The Indian swift breaks all records by traveling at a speed of 172 miles an hour.

Each September the swifts shoot on rapid wings into the South to spend the winter in South America. The migration of swifts for centuries was an unsolved mystery. Long ago folk said these birds buried themselves in the mud of ponds and spent the winter with the frogs. In 1944 Mr. F. C. Lincoln discovered their wintering ground far up the Amazon River Valley in the interior of Brazil.

Illinois Status: Common migrant and summer resident throughout the State.

**Chimney Swifts
(5¼ inches)**

86

TO the brilliant tubes of trumpet flowers there comes a whirring, jewel-like thing, not quite a bird, certainly not an insect — the ruby-throated hummingbird. It comes to all red and orange tubular flowers, from the first dangling nectaries of the early columbines, to the later salvias, jewelweed, cardinal flower, and honeysuckle of gardens and woods. There is no doubt that these colors are favorites, and perhaps remind the hummer of bright flowers in the tropics; yet many a garden is host to hummingbirds that delight in probing into bluebells, tuberoses, or other sweet blossoms that are not red. A buzz, a darting thing, a pulsating, spangled gleam of scarlet on the throat, an emerald gloss on the back — is here, is gone, is back again, the hummer.

The hummingbird is able to fly backward, forward, and up and down on amazing wings which move so fast that human eyes can neither follow nor count their movements.

The nest is a remarkable structure. It is tiny, made of plant silk and spider webs, the whole thing neatly upholstered with pale green lichen "leaves" carefully picked one by one from tree trunk and rock. Here in this little cup may be found two white eggs the size of navy beans and from them emerge a pair of babies resembling nothing so much as wet honeybees. In a little while, however, they grow and feather out and soon go to join their parents. In the lowlands dozens of hummers — the less iridescent young, the green and white females, the red and green males — gather in late summer to feast among the orange honey-pitchers of the jewelweeds. Then, when frost nears in late September, the hummers take wing and buzz off to the South. One day at sundown they set off from the southern coast and shoot across the Gulf of Mexico on a nonstop trip 500 miles long, to breakfast in Yucatan. The ruby-throat is the only hummingbird in eastern North America; the hummingbirds as a family are found only in the New World.

Illinois Status: Fairly common migrant and summer resident throughout the State.

Ruby-throated Hummingbird
(3¾ inches)
(plant: trumpet vine)

O N a summer afternoon when birds are quiet and the pond is host only to dragonflies zooming in the heat, there comes a rattle and a clatter, a quick beat of wings with a snap like sailcloth — a blue-grey bird with rumpled crest and big black beak, the kingfisher. For a long moment it poises on beating wings above the water, then drops like a released harpoon, straight down, sometimes all but submerges, and shaking water, comes up with a small fish. With labored wingbeats the kingfisher flies to a nearby overhanging branch and, with beak thrust into the air, manages somehow to twist the silvery fish around about so that the rasping fins are laid flat and the head is pointed down the bird's throat. A gulp, a slightly popeyed look, and the angler sits quietly for a while until, with that characteristic shout, it flies off in search of more fish.

A kingfisher is a "Tell it to the Marines" sort of bird, a rakish, independent ruler of the shores, one that lives beside almost any body of water. There it stays as late as there is open water and until the last deep hole is glazed and there are no more fish to be found. Then the kingfisher moves just far enough to the South to follow open water and, as soon as the first thaw comes in spring, returns to fish in Illinois ponds.

The nest is made in a bank often near water. With beak and feet especially adapted for this purpose, the bird excavates a long burrow in the bank, and in darkness the young grow up. One day they come forth blinking into the sunshine, to learn the Izaak Walton trade of their parents.

The kingfisher is not a competitor of the fisherman. Except when it adopts a fish hatchery as its feeding pond, it actually is one of those natural controls that helps remove some of the myriads of small fish from our streams and ponds.

The kingfisher is one of the few native birds that has reversed the regular bird coloration schemes. In opposition to the male's trim but subdued coloration of slate blue, black and white, the female has a prominent chestnut-colored wash to her throat and flank bands.

Illinois Status: Fairly common migrant and resident throughout the State. Many remain as permanent residents in the southern part.

Belted Kingfisher (female)
(11 inches)

I N the wild, ecstatic surge of spring, when the sticky buds of the cottonwoods spill fat red catkins and a keen, fresh, growing smell is everywhere, the voice of the flicker steps up the pulse of nature, makes springtime a reality. The voice of the yammering flicker, shouting from treetop or gable, is Spring.

That loud, compelling call is the preliminary to a ridiculous dance which takes place on the crossarm of a telephone pole, on a tree limb, or even on the ground. Two flickers, heads up, tails spread, voices shrill, clamor and yelp, bob up and down, sidle and curtsey in the intensity of their wooing.

The flicker is a brown woodpecker with a white patch on its back, the only brown woodpecker in this part of the country, and one that is always known by its distinctive markings—the white "marshmallow" on the rump, which shows in flight, the red gash on the back of the head, the black mustache-mark of the male, and the black crescent on the breast. The breast is heavily spotted with black, and in flight the wings show bright yellow on their undersides. The flicker is one of the commonest of the woodpeckers; it is at home in town and country, in woods and parks.

Flicker habits are somewhat different from those of most other woodpeckers. Instead of obtaining food entirely from trees, this bird likes nothing better than a busy ant hole on the lawn. There the flicker thrusts down a long beak and a long barbed tongue to entrap the running ants. In the serious matter of nesting, there is often a scatterbrained disregard for woodpecker convention. Normally, a large nest-hole is dug in a tree trunk, but some are bored in barn walls; other nests have been made on a sand beach. Formerly the majority of flickers went south in winter, but now more and more of them stay here throughout the year.

The flicker, the only woodpecker which feeds mainly on lawn insects, is a familiar sight to most people and as a result has many common names and nicknames such as "yellow hammer" and "wickup bird," the latter after the sound of one of its common calls.

Illinois Status: Common migrant and summer resident throughout the State. Common permanent resident in the southern part; a few winter in the central and northern parts in favorable winters.

Yellow-shafted Flicker
(Northern Flicker)
(12 inches)

92

IN deep woods where paths are few and trees are tall, where the plaintive-voiced pewee sings all summer long, and where the sun seldom reaches the ground, the brilliant color-pattern of the red-bellied woodpecker is a splendid sight. A magnificent bird, highly efficient in its own life habits, it is marked with an immaculate white breast, black and white zebra stripes on the back, and glowing orange-vermilion on the head from beak to nape. In the female the forehead is grey. The combination of color is a striking one, conspicuous close at hand or in the Museum, but which in its woodland environment merges with the up-and-downness of bark and trees and shadow. Woodpeckers are like that. They are bright, yet their feather-camouflage hides them, makes them an inconspicuous part of the nice blurring of the forest picture.

The red-belly, a bird of the deep woods in Illinois, seldom ventures away from their protection. Here among the trees a sharp rapping is a good indication of its presence. It flies with that characteristic strong, bounding, woodpecker flight, and utters a loud "chunk, chunk, chunk!" as it goes.

The red-bellied woodpecker is also a bird of the Far South, where it is in constant attendance to the orange groves. It becomes a pest which pecks oranges and sucks their juice. Red-bellies, often called ladder-backs or zebra-birds, are, in spite of their southern connections, very common in Illinois, and in winter often become regular visitors to feeding stations near parks or woods.

As the trees and shrubbery about our homes mature, these ladder-backed woodpeckers become increasingly common at winter feeding stations where they are attracted by both suet and large seeds, especially large sunflower seeds which they take one at a time to a favorite perch, crack open, eat the kernel, and return for another. When no longer hungry they will still continue their trips to the feeder. One was observed to store over five pounds of sunflower seeds in crevices between the bark and wood of an elm tree. This cache was later found and opened up by a fox squirrel.

Illinois Status: Fairly common permanent resident in southern and central parts; less common in northern part although the range seems to be extending northward.

Red-bellied Woodpecker
(9½ inches)
(tree: white oak)

94

A BRIGHT flag of crimson, black, and white flies across the sunshine and takes form as a bird on a telephone pole. That's the red-head, the woodpecker that has forgotten its past and seems to be carving a new future for itself and its posterity. It is well known, usually the first of the tribe to be met by bird-seekers, and yet its habits are confusing. When a bird is a woodpecker, it should act like one, but the red-head quite often does not. Instead of a tree, the red-head enjoys a perch on a telephone wire, and here with tail dangling the woodpecker waits for passing insects, darts out in flycatcher fashion, turns a flip-flop in the air and comes back with a slightly dizzy look. The red-head likes to come down on the highway — down in the middle of the road where there is imminent danger of slaughter — where it picks up grain spilled from wagons, or insects that were missed on the wing. The bird becomes so deeply concerned with its dinner that it forgets to watch for automobiles which approach with such a rush that often the woodpecker, with slow wings not made for a quick takeoff, is borne to the pavement and crushed.

The red-headed woodpecker still nests in tree-holes which are dug with a great deal of labor from the heartwood, or sometimes in dead snags of trees in swamps. Here the white eggs are laid, and here the young emerge and come out into the sunlight. At this stage the young have dark grey, not red, heads, yet are distinguished by those great staring white wing-patches which are the mark of the red-headed woodpecker.

Though the red-headed woodpecker is not as abundant as formerly, it is still a common bird of roadside and large mature oak forest groves. Its alternating body-and-wing pattern of black-white-black is readily observed either when the bird is perched or in flight.

Illinois Status: Permanent resident throughout the State but more common in winter in the southern part than in the north.

Red-headed Woodpecker
(9½ inches)

WHEN April trees send small, tender leaves into the chilly sunshine, and when the earliest trout lilies and violets are blooming among old dead leaves on the woods floor, there comes a strange, meowing bird that clings to birch trunk or poplar bole and tipples sap until almost drunk on this sun-fermented liquor. Early in spring the yellow-bellied sapsucker comes up from southern pine forests, stays a while in Illinois woods, and then, as suddenly as it came, is gone to the North to nest.

No other woodpecker is like the sapsucker. No other woodpecker has a black and red throat, pale yellow front, a long white patch down the black wing, stripes on head and neck, and a patch of red on the forehead. The chisel-beak bores a series of neat little holes in tender bark, preferably in Scotch pine, maple, poplar, or aspen, where the rising sap flows and runs down the trunk. Early insects — flies, bees, anglewing butterflies, and mourning cloaks — gather here to drink sap, while above them in the tree the sapsucker clings with its peculiarly adaptable feet, and drinks, drinks, drinks. After a spree of this sort the sapsucker sometimes cannot fly at all or else goes off at a drunken angle, uttering maudlin meows and queer mad purrs of contentment. The sapsucker returns through Illinois enroute to the South in September and October, and occasionally a few of them spend the winter here.

Illinois Status: Common migrant throughout the State. Fairly common winter resident in southern part.

Yellow-bellied Sapsucker
(9 inches)
(tree: aspen)

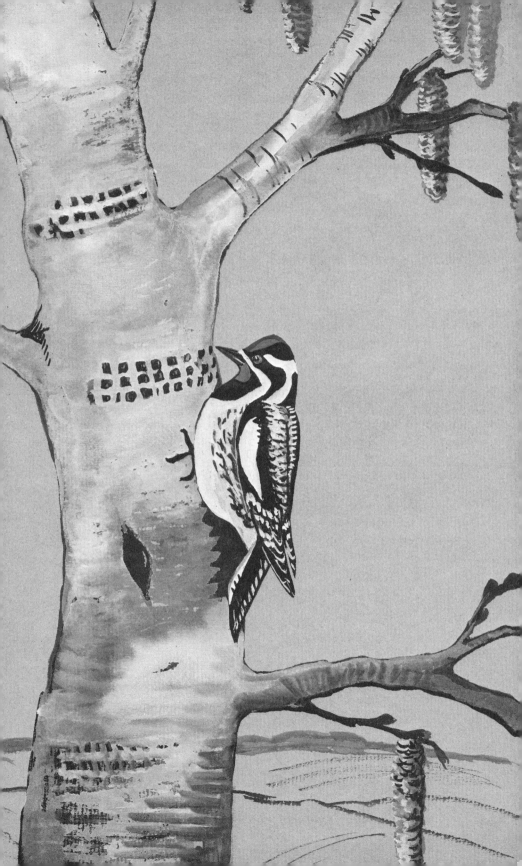

THE downy woodpecker is the one that works the orchards and garden trees all year around; the one that picks up quantities of small but hungry insects; the one that makes itself a necessary, pleasant part of the winter world. The downy is a little black and white bird. The male has a bright red dot on the back of its head, and, like all the woodpeckers which are built to their chosen environment, it has an elongated body, stiff, bracing tail feathers, clinging claws, and a chisel-beak. Inside the beak and head, a three-inch tongue is barbed like an Eskimo spear. When the chisel-beak has bored a hole in a tree, the tongue is thrust inside and impales a grub which the canny woodpecker apparently knew was there.

As the little woodpecker hitches itself up the cold trunk of a sugar maple along the street and braces itself with the stiff tail feathers, the bird now and again utters a sharp "pick!" as it hunts spider eggs in the bark. Or perhaps it is katydid eggs which are found as they were laid in a compact chain; or scale insects on a branch; or a tussock moth cocoon plastered whitely against the bark.

The downy is the woodpecker which most often comes into town, the one which will come promptly and regularly to suet tied against a tree trunk in a city garden. The downy even examines weed stalks left rattling and dry in the winter wind, cleans cornstalks of borers, and makes itself exceedingly useful in the world. Then, its day's work done, the downy gives a sharp call and flies off to its winter bed-tree where a hole is made for long hours of winter sleep.

Another woodpecker has the same color pattern as the downy, but it is fully three inches longer. This is the hairy woodpecker, which, according to some authors, says "peek!" instead of "pick!" and has a longer, heavier beak than that of the downy.

Illinois Status: Common permanent resident throughout the State.

Downy Woodpecker
(6 inches)
(plant: wild parsnip)

THE kingbird likes the highways. Here it sits, pompous white chest thrust out, neat black wings folded, and watches for insects. With a shrill call, a loud snap of the beak, a flip-flop in the air, and a wild flash of wings, the kingbird dashes after an insect and returns, sometimes with the thin wings of a butterfly still protruding from the beak.

The kingbird is a bold, aggressive defender of its nesting territory. With dash and flourish, it chases out kingbirds as well as all other birds — even crows, hawks, and eagles — that come within sight of its perch, be it a weed stalk above the prairie or a dead branch high in a tree. The kingbird is nature's dive bomber, attacking with fury large birds in full flight, striking them on the back over and over again. Its scientific name, *Tyrannus tyrannus*, suggests the bold, pugnacious character. Yet kingbirds have been known to allow other birds, a yellow warbler and a warbling vireo, to nest near them in the same tree without conflict or challenge.

The kingbird is a bird of the open, of the roadsides and sunny uplands and orchards, where a nest of rootlets, grass, and wool is made in a thornbush or apple tree. The kingbird is quick to defend its nest, and in these moments of excitement a small, vivid orange patch on the top of the head flashes brightly — the "crown" of the kingbird.

Illinois Status: Common migrant and summer resident throughout the State.

Eastern Kingbird
(8½ inches)
(tree: apple)

THE crested flycatcher is a crazy clown that bounds and tumbles through the woods in search of insects. A dead tree is its favorite haunt, and in a dead tree, also, perhaps in a gaping hole in the upper trunk, the nest is made. Four or five eggs are laid in a nest at the bottom of the hole. They are a glossy, oiled brown, a mottled olive color, shiny as well-polished Easter eggs. And in the nest or sometimes around the entrance to the hole the crested flycatcher, with madcap ingenuity, sometimes drapes a castoff snakeskin, or, failing that, substitutes fish scales or onionskins inside the nest. Today one may find a discarded plastic wrapper of a cigarette package replacing the traditional snakeskin. Not all crested flycatchers add this finishing touch to the nest, but they do have that clownish habit of turning flip-flops, of screeching, of tumbling headlong through the woods. All flycatchers have something of this unpredictability, but the great crested seems to be the champion.

A long, sleek, well-built bird with a reflective look in its big white-rimmed eyes, sits upon a dead tree in a clearing. Suddenly there is a throat-rending screech. The flycatcher is catapulted into the air, turns a double somersault, comes back, wild-eyed, to its perch. The puffy head is crested now; in the bright eyes there is a wild look almost of madness. A slight gulp — the captured insect is gone — and the flycatcher is once more on the alert.

The crested flycatcher is our largest common flycatcher. It has the typical erect flycatcher silhouette and the large gaping mouth to scoop in insects in flight. Essentially it is a grey bird with a wash of yellow on the breast and a prominent chestnut color which flashes in flight from the tail and wings.

Illinois Status: Common migrant and summer resident throughout the State.

**Great Crested Flycatcher
(9 inches)**

WHEN spring is still so far away that ice sometimes forms at night in sheltered inlets and when the pussy willows are only beginning to be host to a few half-frozen bees, a grey-brown bird comes to sit on a willow twig beside the bridge. The earliest stone flies, the guzzling bees, leftover flies, and dancing mosquitoes all come as welcome food for the phoebe on those early spring days — cold, wet days for one depending upon tender insect life for a livelihood.

The phoebe is the first flycatcher to return in spring, coming to lakeshores, summer cottages, bridge sites, woodland edges or clearings — always to open places where the early spring sun first brings out the flying insects on which the phoebe is dependent. This alert little bird, with its gaping mouth, gobbles up insects in flight, catching them with a distinct and audible click of the bill.

Perched on an open branch, the phoebe sits in the typical flycatcher pose — erect and alert, with a slight crest and a white puffy chest—the only small flycatcher without wing bars or eyering. Wait but a few moments and it will clearly tell you its name. "Phoe-be — phoe-be," it will repeat ever so distinctly, and with each call it flips its tail up and down. The call and the habit of tail-wagging will identify it. The chickadee has a similar call, but the chickadee clearly whistles "fee-bee" while the phoebe says it more as a nasal word rather than a whistle.

The phoebe builds a rather substantial nest under a cottage eave, on a bridge beam, or sometimes on a rock ledge — the nest securely plastered with mud and lined with grass. There may be four or five young; and they too will consume their own weight or more in insects each day.

Illinois Status: Common migrant and summer resident throughout the State. In favorable weather a few may winter in the southern part.

Eastern Phoebe
(7 inches)
(tree: pussy willow)

WHEN night is still deep black, and in that three-o'clock feeling of early morning the air is damp and still and cool, the whippoor-will has usually stopped its hiccoughing and the owls are silent. But now, at a few minutes past three, a sweet, sad, thin whistle comes through the woods, three notes, then two that slur. The wood pewee is awake in the darkness, has opened the day with its call. A bird is awake, but the world still sleeps, and so perhaps the pewee dozes again, or moves about impatiently and preens its feathers as it waits for that narrow orange line over in the east to light the day as the summer sun comes up.

The pewee is the bird that sings first in the summer predawn, the one that starts the robins to carolling and the catbird to smirking and giggling in the dew-soaked crabapple thickets. The pewee is a flycatcher of the deep woods and parks. Its plaintive voice is heard all day long, from earliest morning often until late at night. The song may vary in pattern throughout the day, yet it is essentially that same thin, distinctive call — "Pee-aw-wee." From a nearby perch the call comes again and again, elusive like the voice of the ventriloquist.

A slim grey bird with two white wing bars and no eye-ring, the pewee is most often seen perched on a dead twig in a clearing in the woods. It sits quietly, but ever alert, in typical flycatcher silhouette, erect, chesty, with a slight crest, and scanning the air from the open perch. It feeds entirely on flying insects — hundreds of them each day.

Only by the rarest chance, however, is the beautiful little nest discovered. Like that of the hummingbird, it is a nest upholstered with fine little lichen "leaves"; it is made chiefly of rootlets instead of cotton and spider webs and is situated on a horizontal limb high in the forest. Nearby, the parent birds, both alike in color and pattern, spend their time catching winged insects that flutter through the clearing and among the leaves.

Illinois Status: Common migrant and summer resident throughout the State.

Eastern Wood Pewee
(6½ inches)
(tree: red birch)

108

OUT across the wet fields of last year's stubble, and among the sodden, dead pasture grass in late winter, there comes a sweet, tinkling song, repeated over and over again, sometimes before sunrise, then again as the chill February dusk closes down. There are birds out there, birds oblivious to cold wind and icy field — the horned larks.

Horned larks are flatland birds, the color of dust and dead grass, a blending of tan, grey, and off-white, with distinctive, sharp black markings on the face and a wash of yellow on the throat. In spring as the larks run along the road, or perch singing on a bean stalk, two little black feather horns stand erect on the head. Usually these lie flat, but as spring comes on they are raised high in the joy of song.

From a wet, unplowed field a small bird flies up, up, almost out of sight, tinkling a song as it hovers high in the air, and then drops down like a plummet to the field where a small lark waits in what must surely be admiration for the singer. In this habit of sky-song the horned lark resembles the skylarks singing over England when spring is on the apple trees, but the skylark's song is longer, richer, and more musical. American horned larks are closely related to the European skylark.

The horned lark is joined in winter by the northern variety which, in search of small seeds, all day walks patiently in big flocks through snow and stubble. With them may be Lapland longspurs. They and the northern larks go north in March. Then the prairie cousins build a simple grass nest in a slight hollow in the field, and sometimes even before snow is past the eggs are laid. Late cold snaps seldom disturb the horned larks, and evening once more hears their tinkling songs that come across the wet, cold fields.

The horned lark originally was a native of the short grass prairies of the West and even the long grass prairies of Illinois. The clearing of the big woods and the cultivation and development of the land opened up a whole new range for these birds. They have adapted well to man-made environments of fields, roadsides, airports, and golf courses and are now thought to be one of the most abundant nesting species in Illinois. Their range has been extended all the way to the East Coast and north into New England.

Illinois Status: Common permanent resident of open areas throughout the State.

Horned Lark
(7¾ inches)

SWALLOWS in the air, swallows in long lines on the telephone wires, swallows that gather by hundreds in the dead trees of swamps and river lowlands — by these signs it is known that autumn approaches. And even though August may show scant sign of coming change, and there is no evidence of any crimson bough on buckeye tree or maple, the swallows nevertheless herald a changing season. They gather together near water and wait for the call that sends them southward. They are among the first birds to leave, and when they go, the lakes are bereft of darting wings, the river swamps vacant of the glint of steely green backs in sunshine. Not until another April will there be swallows.

The white-breasted swallows — the tree swallow, bank swallow and rough-winged swallow — are among the six kinds of swallows that may be found in Illinois during spring and fall migration.

The tree swallow is known by its immaculate white throat and breast and its dark back. The males show brilliant iridescence of green, blue and purple. Tree swallows are common in northern Illinois and northward where they remain to nest, often in colonies like martins. They particularly like nesting holes near water. A bluebird house on a fence post set in the lake or a small edition of a martin house (with $1\frac{1}{2}''$ openings) mounted near the beach is almost certain to attract them.

The bank swallows and rough-winged swallows are found locally throughout the State wherever the soil conditions of banks are sufficiently light and easy to excavate with the tiny feet and bills of these burrow-nesting birds. The bank swallows are easily recognized by their white throats and gray throat bands, while the rough-winged swallow has an all-grey throat but white chest.

Swallows are a personification of grace as they swoop back and forth feeding on flying insects — sometimes low over water, road, or field and, at other times, high in the air. Wherever insects are flying, the flocks of swallows soar and dip with perfect control on long tapered wings.

Illinois Status: All are common migrants. The bank and rough-winged are common summer residents wherever there are favorable nesting banks. The tree swallow is a common summer resident in the north and uncommon resident in the south.

left: Bank Swallow   (5¼ in.)
right: two Tree Swallows (6 in.)

112

THE barn swallow is a shining, satiny prince of a bird, gay, living color and grace that skims over pasture pond and dewy field, or twitters around the barn and over the drab contrast of the hog sheds. Barn swallows are masters of flight and are famous for their long "swallow-tails," from which have been named certain coattails and butterfly wings. The barn swallow's tail is long and deeply forked, with a row of oval white spots around the curve. The wings and upperparts are glossy dark blue. The throat and breast bear the colors of sunset, a blending of rosy apricot that shades to pale yellow and white near the tail.

Barn swallows like to nest on rafters in barns and under the eaves of porches and summer cottages. The open barn door is usually used for entry, but when this is closed, a small opening in the barn wall is large enough for a doorway. The swallows come flying at a great rate of speed straight toward the blank wall. They chatter gutturally as they come, and at the moment when it seems they must crash, there is a slight swerve, and they are gone. Their aim is true; into the barn they fly, one by one, and skim to their nests, each to its own. The nests are mud and grass structures set in a row on rafter or beam. The material is gathered awkwardly from the ground — picked up bit by bit by birds whose feet through lack of use have become small and weak.

The barn swallow continues to prosper in association with man; but the cliff swallow, well known to our grandparents, is now found only in a very few isolated colonies. Cliff swallows, like the barn swallows, are dark and satiny with beautiful chestnut and buffy underparts. They lack the barn swallow's long "swallow-tails" and have a prominent, light-chestnut forehead and rump patch.

Once they plastered their strange round hollow mud nests to rock cliffs often above water. The early farm buildings of logs or rough-sawed lumber with irregular, uneven surfaces proved an excellent substitute for the rocky cliffs, and many farms supported great colonies of cliff swallows. As the construction of farm buildings changed from rough-sawed to smooth-sawed and painted lumber with no irregularities on which to plaster their nests, the cliff swallows have again retreated to rough vertical rock surfaces. Although nesting colonies are few and far between in Illinois, these birds may often be seen among concentrations of migrating swallows.

Illinois Status: Barn swallow is a common migrant and summer resident. Cliff swallow is an uncommon migrant and locally restricted summer resident.

Barn Swallow
(7 inches)

THERE is a contralto chattering, a flutter of shiny blue-black wings around the big martin box in the yard. It is April, and the purple martins, largest of the swallows, have returned for the summer. They fill the sunlight with pleasant sounds, flash high into the sky, or, early in the morning, visit the shores of the park pond. The short legs of swallows are not adapted to walking; so they are very awkward. They perch well on a wire or branch but seldom walk on the ground. Yet, martins do come down on the ground to dust-bathe and gather bits of dry grass and dabs of mud in their beaks as nest-building material. These birds have almost completely shifted their nesting from natural cavities to man-made martin houses. Though awkward on the ground, in the air they are grace personified. They are on the wing all day and at sunset come down out of the sky for the last time, chatter throatily for a few minutes, and then retire for a brief summer night. They are up and away very early, even before sunrise, for the twittering of purple martins can be heard over town amid that first united carolling of robins at four o'clock.

The purple martin is known by its entirely dark appearance, a glossy blue-black with a purple glint. The female is dark above with a greyish breast. The martin's large size and uniform dark color both above and below distinguish it from all other swallows found in Illinois.

The dark male martins arrive with the first warm balmy southern breezes in April. They are hardy birds and may appear as soon as warm days bring out the flying insects upon which they feed. Disaster sometimes strikes these early returning swallows; for after three or four cold days without flying insects, the martins become so weakened that they can no longer fly and so they starve. However, they are skilled hunters and will often seek flying insects in the warm rising air currents above a highway, pond, protected bay or sunny side of a woods.

It is fortunate that the females do not arrive until about two weeks after the males, for they are not so often overtaken by disastrous weather. The colonial and polygamous nature of these swallows usually effects a quick recovery of any serious population losses.

These birds are readily attracted to new residential areas where the utility wires and television antennas of the treeless subdivisions make good perches, affording the residents the cheerful contact with bird life before the growth of shrubbery and trees brings in the usual array of birds.

Illinois Status: Common migrant and summer resident throughout the State.

Purple Martin
(8 inches)

THE blue jay is a bold, blue, exquisite, rowdy, owl-chasing bounder, a dashing beauty — common, yet one of the most splendidly colored of American birds. Blue is a rare color in feathers, and the jay is one of the most beautiful of blue birds. A flash of sky-colored wings marked with black and white, a flare of a blue and white fantail, a twitch of a blue crest—that's the jay. Its voice varies from the hoarse shout of the mischief-maker with its prey in sight, to the sweet, unutterably tender, throaty trills and murmurings of spring. A shrill clarion call rings through the oakwoods; a musical gurgle is almost always accompanied by a bounding dance. But when a gang of jays, out for fun, trouble, or the love of spring sunshine, comes clanging and tootling through the woods, then let slumbering owls beware. Jays love an owl chase. Trace the noise to its source, and in a tree there may sit a big, befuddled, barred owl that submits to insults and epithets flung by the ribald gang. They will also descend noisily on a squirrel, a crow, a fox, or other intruders in their domain.

The jay in all its crisp, fastidious beauty is a permanent resident that spends its time in woods, parks, farms, and towns. It is essentially a bird of the trees, yet it is often found within a block or two of the business district of a large city. There in gardens the jay hunts for food scraps, teases other birds, sometimes robs their nests, and in winter makes a brilliant spot of color against the snow.

Blue jays are exceptionally well adapted to a wide variety of habitats, climates and foods. They live exuberantly the whole year round from the Canadian North Woods to the Gulf Coast. They will eat nuts, grains, fruit, eggs, insects and table scraps. They can hold hard seeds and nuts against a perch with their feet and pound them open with their beaks, or they may bury acorns which they never find again. If they locate a supply of large seeds such as corn or sunflower seeds they will piggishly pick up a gullet-full and fly off to a protected perch where they deposit them and crack them open one at a time for the nutmeat within.

Illinois Status: Common throughout Illinois during the entire year.

**Blue Jay
(11¾ inches)**

THEY come across the orange sunset on a winter afternoon — crows heading to their roosting places for the long cold night. They come like black-etched figures on a Chinese print. They fly high, in twos, in threes, in a scattered flock, inked against the glow. And next morning at dawn they stretch their wings, utter rasping caws that somehow belong to the stubble fields and the clear, cold, lemon light of dawn, and off they go, low now, on the lookout for breakfast as they spread to their feeding grounds.

Crows undoubtedly may be a nuisance, may cause some damage to corn, crops, and young birds. Hate may be heaped upon their ebony heads, a price upon their strong wings, yet they are still a part of the prairie landscape. They are a part of the plowed fields, where they come down to devour grubs and insects turned over by the plow. Crows are a part of the river shore and the lake ice where they eat dead fish left to decay. They take the place of vultures in cleaning up the mangled bodies of the night's kill of animals on the highway. Crows are a definite part of the Illinois picture — jet black, independent, wild birds whose intelligence has risen with necessity as it has been matched against the human enemy.

The prairie landscape would be empty without those black crows beating across the sunset, those raucous, derisive voices on a pleasant day in spring. There would somehow be a lack in the meaning of corn crop and wheat field, no matter how successful they might be, without crows to be reviled — and, in spite of their habits, admired. And as our understanding of the creatures of the wild increases, our tolerance and respect tends to replace the almost vengeful hate of man for these wildlings that have not only survived but prospered in spite of man's persecution.

In Illinois the crow has been removed officially from that strange limbo with vermin. Like all other native wild birds, it is now protected by law; a license or permit is required to shoot or in any other way destroy crows in Illinois.

Illinois Status: Common permanent residents throughout the State. Often more abundant in winter.

**Common Crows
(19 inches)**

I T is difficult to explain how small birds survive in extremely low temperatures. Yet on a bitter day, twenty degrees or so below zero, with a biting wind and a thick blanketing of dry, powdery snow underfoot, the chickadees are as merry as on a day in May, and they are much more friendly. The wind may be ruthless as a knife, the air so sharp it hurts to breathe it; yet there comes a contented little chittering somewhere in the trees, a rattling, businesslike little "dee-dee-dee-dee!"—a small voice full of supreme hope and courage that chatters confidently into the wind. The black-capped chickadee, with its inky bib and bonnet, cheerfully hunts for small sleeping insects and insect eggs and, in the face of stark winter, whistles merrily.

The chickadee is everywhere a favorite, not only on a winter day when stamina and endurance are at stake but at other seasons too. There is boundless energy expended in carrying out chips from an old woodpecker hole one day in April and in gathering up feathers to fill the hole with a feather bed. It seems that young chickadees might almost smother in that fluffy bed, yet they finally emerge with the same cheerful personalities as their parents.

The chickadee stays the year around in parks, woods, and cemeteries and in winter often comes into town where a feeding stand with ample suet and sunflower seeds brings chickadees as daily guests. They seem to fear no extreme of cold. The long, loose feathers cover a thick layer of extra-warm down which, when puffed out, makes a warm-air space to keep the little body snug on the coldest night. With enough food to keep body heat at its usual high temperature, no chickadee will freeze to death.

Enough food is quite an order for the tiny bundle of energy called a chickadee; for with a heart racing along at 400 to 600 beats per minute, the little body heats to a normal temperature of 114° F. To sustain that high-speed, hot motor, the bird must consume two to three times its body weight each day. No wonder every waking moment of its busy, cheerful, inquisitive day is spent in a constant search for food.

Illinois Status: Common permanent resident in the northern and central sections but usually replaced by the similar Carolina chickadee in the southern part.

Black-capped Chickadee
(5¼ inches)
(tree: white pine)

A SMALL, trim, mouse-grey personality — a sharp grey topknot, a fussing, fluttering, busy nature — that's the tufted titmouse. It lives in parks, woods, and towns where its cheerful whistle greets the passerby with boundless enthusiasm and makes even the dogs take notice. It is easy to imitate that clear whistle and an immediate answer from the nearest titmouse usually follows. There is a fussy squeaking, a flutter of grey wings, and the titmouse is off to investigate this sound which seems so much like an orthodox titmouse call, but with a subtle difference. Usually more than one bird will respond; so the whistling hiker may often make his walk in the park or woods into a veritable procession of birds.

The titmouse weathers all the seasons with equal good humor. In winter the feathers are fluffed out for warmth and give the titmouse a chubby, well-fed look which is very agreeable to meet in the stark cold and silence of the winter woods. The titmouse is one of the few winter singers. It makes the world more friendly for its carol, the day more pleasant because of an unquenchably cheerful disposition.

Distinctive though it is, however, the titmouse has often been confused with the cedar waxwing, because these two are the only birds of this size which are grey and have a topknot. But the waxwing's lazy, languid personality is very different from the nervous energy and good spirits of the titmouse. The waxwing has a band of yellow across the tail, red on the wingtips; the titmouse is all grey, except for a wash of chestnut-brown on the sides. Although the two birds may appear quite similar at first glance, their characters are entirely different. That of the titmouse is outstanding for its perennial good humor.

Actually the titmouse is closely related to the chickadee whose habits are very similar. The titmouse even has a call quite like that of the chickadee, his smaller cousin. This can be quite confusing to the beginner until he learns to detect the more nasal quality of the titmouse.

Illinois Status: Permanent resident throughout the State but less common in northern than in central and southern parts.

Tufted Titmouse
(6 inches)
(tree: buckeye)

LISTEN for gnomish laughter among the trees. Listen: it is high and shrill, guttural and sardonic, a small guffaw, its maker not in sight. Look again. Examine the tree trunks there in the park where only the faintest vestige of spring is making itself known by swelling willow buds and maple flowers. And there it is — a neat, grey and white bird running headlong down a tree trunk, and laughing. Some call the sound simply a "yank, yank, yank!" but this is dull language for one so witty. Perhaps it is more like a derisive "nya-nya-nya!" and then a shrill, comical, "ha-ha-ha-ha-ha!" laughed like a mirthful triphammer. This is the white-breasted nuthatch, an all-year-around bird of the woods, one whose laughter in early spring is one of the most entertaining sounds in the wild.

The nuthatches are known at once by their curious habit of running about with a total disregard for the laws of gravity. They skitter about on the underside of a horizontal limb, run head first down a tree trunk and usually choose not to follow the more staid, upright position of ascending a tree. The beak is chisel-like, somewhat tilted for better efficiency in digging under bark for the insects and spider eggs which the nuthatch prefers for food. In England, a similar bird was named "nuthack," and the American nuthatch, likewise, often tucks a sunflower seed in a crevice of bark and hacks it open.

The white-breasted nuthatch is known by its shiny black cap, white front and cheeks, a wash of pale brown on the sides, a stubby black and white tail, and grey-blue wings and back. It, too, is a common attendant at winter feeding stations mingling with chickadees and titmice in the scramble for sunflower seeds and suet. After eating its fill, it will then carry off seeds and suet to store in every crevice and crack of nearby trees. This habit has the most wonderful effect, for soon every tree in the neighborhood is converted into a feeding station for some of the more timid winter feeders, especially the little brown creepers that seldom venture onto man-made feeders.

A northern cousin, the red-breasted nuthatch, is showing up with increasing regularity at winter feeding stations in central and northern Illinois.

Illinois Status: Common permanent resident throughout the State.

White-breasted Nuthatch
(5¾ inches)
(tree: sweet gum)

IN winter when trees along the street stand chill and leafless below a leaden sky of snow, there comes a thin squeak. Bare though the trees are, the maker of the sound might go unseen, except for a flash of brown wings swooping from the upper part of the tree, down to the bottom of the next. A flash of brown, and a small, slim body is clapped against a tree trunk and immediately becomes all but invisible against the blurring camouflage of bark. The brown creeper moves so quietly and blends so completely with the tree trunks that it is our least known common winter resident.

From October to April the creeper is as much at home in city elms as in the woods and parks. Wherever there are trees, even in the city square or between apartment houses, the little bird may find them. In spring the brown creeper goes far northward to nest; only when the push of winter shoves it out of its summer home does the bird move south where in Illinois it becomes an integral part of winter trees.

The brown creeper is essentially a bird of the tree trunks; its markings, all up-and-down streakings, are a good imitation of bark. The beak is rather long and curved, good for picking out a spider egg from crack or crevice; a long tongue flicks out to lick up a morsel of suet. Unlike the woodpeckers which hitch themselves straight up a tree trunk, the brown creeper climbs in a spiral. Like the woodpeckers, the creeper seldom moves backward because its sharp tail feathers catch uncomfortably in the bark.

The brown creeper moves through the woods in a very definite pattern. It flies to the base of a tree and climbs up searching for food, then flies to the base of the next tree, always flying down and climbing up in this continual rhythm of its systematic search.

In spring the simple squeak which distinguishes the brown creeper is sometimes surprisingly improved by a song which might be that of Bewick's wren or myrtle warbler — a small masterpiece of song which is heard infrequently, when the zest of spring makes even silent creatures vocal.

Illinois Status: Common migrant and winter resident.

Brown Creeper
(5½ inches)

128

LONG ago the house wrens lived in little caves and crannies on the faces of cliffs, or in hollow trees and deserted woodpecker and owl holes. "Troglodytes," the Latin name for wren, means simply "cave-dweller," but when the kindly hand of man offered a varied assortment of birdhouses for their express use, most of the wrens gave up their cave-dwelling habits and moved to the haunts of men.

Sometimes, however, even the finest and most elaborate of houses does not suit the finicky, tilt-tailed, spluttering Jenny. Off it goes, flipping about, bright eyes looking everywhere for a better place. Consequently sometimes a pocket of an old coat hung on a back-porch nail is chosen; or a tin can lodged in a crotch of a tree; or a spidery jug; an upturned cemetery urn, or an old hat fastened to a battered scarecrow.

When the selection is made, the busy wrens clean out the place and spend several days carrying in beak-fulls of twigs and grass, a few feathers, and sometimes an old nail or two just for variety. Here in this mass of rubbish the pink-brown, speckled eggs are laid.

The house wren has long since become a part of human habitation, a busy member of orchard, garden, or farm. Even in hot weather that lively song runs on all day, bubbling from the little brown wren that droops its expressive tail and sings.

In March and April sometimes a slender grey-brown wren, the Bewick's, may appear about a farmyard or open residential area. The prominent white eyebrow and white outer fringe of the long, rounded tail help identify this noisy yet elusive wren. Though it will return from year to year to a chosen nesting locale, it seems nowhere common, except perhaps in southern Illinois.

Illinois Status: House wren is a common migrant and summer resident throughout the State. Bewick's wren is an uncommon permanent resident in the southern part and may be extending its range northward, appearing occasionally in central and rarely in northern Illinois.

top: Bewick's Wren   (5 in.)
bottom: House Wren   (5 in.)
          (plant: young grape)

ON a winter day that is tight with cold — when the creek is frozen hard, with a pattern of snow blown upon it, and when birds are few and silently busy among the weeds — there may come a queer, loud, winding-up sound followed by a ringing burst of song. Here on a winter's day, no matter how cold, and no matter how quiet other birds may be, the Carolina wren sings enthusiastically and well. Its call has a loud ringing cardinal-like quality. "Tea-kettle—tea-kettle—tea-kettle," it seems to say as it rings out from a brushy thicket. So secretive are these birds in their habits that they are more often heard than seen.

'The burst of music is succeeded by a loud, throaty chirruping, and with a wary eye, a big brown wren hops out along an overhanging ledge, or over a log and through the winter-whitened weeds. It comes in a series of energetic little bounces, muttering to itself and eyeing everything, with pert tail in the air and quizzical eyebrow cocked. The Carolina wren is a friendly bird that is often overwhelmed by curiosity. It is plump and cinnamon-brown, with that sharp white eyebrow, and is our largest wren, the brightest in color, and perhaps most easily distinguished from other members of this lively family. A neat tail that is thrust straight in the air except during a song and the bubbling quality of the music, both proclaim the Carolina wren.

It is a bird of the deep woods and parks and prefers to live near watercourses. It builds a large nest of sticks and grass under a ledge or in a tree-hollow, although occasionally a garage or shed also may be host to these wrens during the nesting season. The Carolina wren is the only permanent resident of this family in Illinois.

This large wren can be attracted to a winter feeding tray with a suet cake mixed with peanut butter and small seeds. At the feeder, it will assume a threatening pose toward other birds, especially other Carolina wrens. It will drop its tail and point its long sharp beak at those other birds which are often a yard or more away. Even the ubiquitous titmouse stays away until this wren has finished feeding.

Illinois Status: Common permanent resident in central and southern parts but uncommon to rare in the north.

Carolina Wren
(5½ inches)

THE mockingbird is a trim, grey and white individualist with a Voice. On a day in spring when the mocker is feeling well, it mounts to a telephone pole or twig tip, droops that long, sleek tail, and often without opening the beak, sings — sings in a dozen different ways, mocks all the birds it knows, improvises with infinite variations and trillings. Sometimes in the ecstacy of spring, the mocker darts up from its perch, turns a flip-flop in midair, and, still singing, comes down again. It likes to sing in moonlight, not only in the South where it is famous, but in Illinois. When the June moon is large and full, the mockingbird sings at midnight — a dreamy, ethereal, far-off melody sung to the stars.

Mockingbirds are fond of osage orange hedges, fences, farms, and sunny, dry uplands full of thornbushes. Cities know mockers that sometimes spend the winter in gardens and visit feeding stands, along with the usual jays, cardinals, and sparrows, and eat chopped apples and table scraps. The nest is built in a syringa bush, a lilac, or a hedge, and the young are reared in the hot Illinois summer, just as young mockers are reared all over Georgia. There is no difference between the Illinois mockingbird and those which have become so famous among the cotton fields and crepe myrtles.

The mockingbird is recognized by its sleek greyness and long dark tail which has white on either side and is often spread to a fan. On each wing a large white patch shows in flight. Unlike the shrike, for which the mocker is sometimes mistaken, there are no black markings on head and face.

Beautiful songbirds, they tend to be pugnacious, aggressive, and dominant, taking complete charge of the bird world in whatever yard they adopt. Even squirrels, cats and dogs keep a wary eye out for these aggressive dive bombers.

The mockingbirds have long been well established in southern Illinois, in the land of giant magnolias and brilliant crepe myrtle, but they are steadily expanding their range northward, seemingly moving into new areas in winter and remaining to nest in summer.

Illinois Status: Common permanent resident in southern Illinois. Uncommon in the central section and a relatively rare summer resident in the north.

Mockingbird
(Northern Mockingbird)
(10½ inches)
(tree: tulip)

THE catbird is dark slate-grey with a black cap and a red-brown patch under its tail. The black eyes are unusually bright; they seem to spy out everything, while the voice, a jumbled medley of sweet music, catcalls, squeaks, and mockings, seems quite unable to separate anything clearly. There in the bush the bird gurgles and giggles and peeks out with a clownish eye. When the neighbor's cat comes along, or when something else arouses the catbird to more than passing interest, one hears that familiar mewing sound which gave the bird its name.

The nest is made of thin twigs and rootlets, placed at about eye level in a tangled bush. Here the four or five shiny green-blue eggs are laid in June and here the young emerge. They soon hop forth, with their ridiculously abbreviated tails, to find the birdbath which their parents long since had claimed in the name of all catbirds. They like to bathe often and well, and the young, inheriting this cleanly habit, become bath-conscious at an early age.

In song, the catbird is not easily distinguished from the brown thrasher, its cousin, yet if each phrase is repeated carefully twice or more, it's the thrasher singing. If there is seldom anything repeated and if music flows in a rollicking, tumbling, incoherent stream, then it's the catbird, back again from a winter in Florida. For nearly five months, from late April to September, the catbird is a part of the garden, an entertaining portion of the summer.

The catbird, in spite of its bubbling enthustiastic song, is the shy member of the mockingbird family. One of the more common birds of shrubbery or thicket, it tends to stay out of sight until it has become quite accustomed to the surroundings.

Illinois Status: Common migrant and summer resident throughout the State. A few remain over winter in the southern part.

Catbird
(Gray Catbird)
(9 Inches)
(plant: wild rose)

WHEN it's April and the redbuds bloom, when there are rosy peach trees, scented white plum blossoms, and new-leaved willows everywhere, there comes one of the grandest songs of spring. In the top of a poplar, or out in the lilac bush, the brown thrasher sits and sings, and its long body is eloquent with song.

The brown thrasher owes its virtuosity to its kinship with the mockingbird. Like the latter, its song is made up of mimickings and improvisations, of catcalls and grace notes, of original compositions and improvements over the songs of other birds. Listen to the song: there's the bobwhite, the bluebird, a purple martin, a redwing by the pond, a burst of wren-music, the cacophony of a guinea hen, the soft love-notes of a cardinal — and they all issue from this one bird's throat. Yet there is an original melody, too, which is indescribable. The thrasher is further known because it repeats every phrase at least twice, as if to fix it forever in its mind.

Some people have called the thrasher the "brown thrush," yet the thrasher is more like the mockingbird or wren, to which it is related, than like the meek-eyed thrush of the robin tribe. The thrasher is cinnamon-brown above, with a long tail, a long yellow-brown beak, a fierce yellow eye, and long brown streaks on the cream-colored breast. A thrush is plump, has round brown spots, a short tail, brown eyes, and a short brown beak. And no thrush, however eloquent, can match the thrasher for the sheer joy of living when it sings in the plum tree up against a fresh, clean, April sky.

The nest is made in a bush or thorn tree, in upland pasture, thicket, or garden, in park, cemetery, or farm. It is a large nest, made of many entwined thorny twigs and rootlets, in which the four or five creamy eggs, thickly speckled with brown, are laid.

Few birds will stay on the nest so close to threatened danger as will a female thrasher. Reluctant to leave, although the throbbing of her heart can be seen in her entire body, she will peck at the intruder as readily as any brooding hen. As the thrashers hop about in the open yard, they are as bold as catbirds are secretive.

Illinois Status: Common migrant and summer resident throughout the State. A few remain to winter more commonly in southern than in central or northern sections.

Brown Thrasher
(11½ inches)
(tree: wild plum)

THE robin is the one that follows the wood pewee in the early morning bird chorus. With the first hint of dawn, even while that silent, dewy chill is on the world and only a faint slit of light shows in the east, the robins rouse themselves and begin to sing. Folk who awaken early listen as the chorus rolls over city streets and silent houses. Here is one vast song of carolling robins, one which begins somewhere at the edge of things and covers the town as with a blanket of song. Then, as other birds wake and sing, the robins slack their efforts; and, although they may sing as individuals many times throughout the day and again at sunset, there will not be another great chorus until next morning at four o'clock.

Robins are sociable and trusting, their schedule unpredictable. Much is heard about the proverbial "first robin," and the things it foretells, yet all winter long in bottomlands and deep woods, small flocks of robins live contentedly in cold weather. They stay as long as there is food, and robin food is generally abundant — greenbrier berries, dried elderberries, old red haws, crabapples, and dried wild grapes. There many robins stay, and sometimes one or two venture into town in January and are heralded with glad shouts and a column in the newspapers — "First robin predicts an early spring!"

Later, in February and March, the first migrant robins come up from southern Illinois and the Kentucky bottoms, stay a while, and then move northward with the spring, and are replaced by other detachments from still farther south. These later birds settle down and build a comfortable mud nest in the crotch of a tree in a city yard; here they lay greenish-blue eggs when April has barely begun. There are two or three broods each summer. In late autumn, their feathers renewed, with white tail-tips shining like taillights in the migration flight, the robins head south again—or stay close by. Who knows?

Illinois Status: Abundant migrant and summer resident. Winter resident in southern part.

Robin
(American Robin)
(10 inches)
(tree: chokeberry)

IN the cool green gloom of bottomland woods, where the river moves somberly between its muddy banks and the river maples grow high, the wood thrush comes in late April to nest. Here in these lonely woods it lives contentedly all the long hot Illinois summer and fills the late afternoon with music. The sun goes down to the piping of piccolos, the ringing of bells, the twittering of flutes, as the wood thrush mounts to a high twig and with deliberation and calmness sings to the vanishing day. And they who stand below to listen hear the bell-like, golden purity of the thrush's voice and marvel at its beauty.

Yet the wood thrush is not confined to the river woods. It likes the parks and wooded streets near the parks and even comes far into town where trees and garden offer sanctuary. Here on a rainy day the song is pure and lovely — somehow on such a day the noise of traffic is hushed while the wood thrush chants.

The thrush is somewhat smaller than a robin and is a bright cinnamon brown above, brighter on the head, with a snow-white breast evenly marked with distinct, round, black spots which distinguish this bird from all other thrushes.

The hermit thrush, pictured with the wood thrush on the opposite page, is a small, shy migrant that annually spends a few days or more in Illinois woods and gardens. It is distinguished by a grey-brown back and red-brown tail, a white breast lightly marked with brown spots, and an indistinct white eye-ring. Usually upon alighting the hermit thrush deliberately lifts its tail and drops it. Rarely on a spring morning in Illinois the hermit thrush sings as it does in its cool northern woods.

The hermit thrush is a good representative of some five kinds of small thrushes that move quietly through Illinois each spring and fall; and each, as it reaches the latitude and habitat of its nesting, becomes one of the sterling performers of the songbird world. The beautiful reedy song of each kind in its own territory is often referred to as the most beautiful song of the woods.

Illinois Status: Wood thrush is a common migrant and summer resident throughout Illinois woodlands. Hermit thrush is usually found only during spring and fall migration.

top:	Wood Thrush	(8¼ in.)
bottom:	Hermit Thrush	(7½ in.)
	(plant:	moonseed)

142

THERE comes a plaintive, throaty warble on the late February air, a bright velvet-blue creature that flies down from the blossoming maple to the sodden grass where as yet there is no trace of green. Bluebirds are back from the South and spring is surely here.

Long ago in the Massachusetts Colony which had somehow survived that first cruel winter at Plymouth, the people were hungry for the sight and sound of spring. The harsh pines on the sand hills thrashed in a strong southeast wind off the Atlantic. Gulls along the shore screamed and dipped, and then—one day in late winter the children, who had ventured a little way from the cabins, came running home to tell their parents about the blue robin they had seen. It was so much like the beloved English robin they had left behind in the hedgerows of Old England, yet this one was blue — bluer than the ocean, bluer even than the sky! And so the Pilgrims named it the blue robin, our bluebird which today is greeted with almost the same thrill and pleasure as the Pilgrims felt at sight of it.

Now, as then, the bluebird is the sign of spring. One day it suddenly appears on a fence post or apple twig, and, like a blue feather, drops down, picks up something, and is back on its perch again.

Indians said that the bluebird was made of blue sky, red earth, and the remnants of snow left over from winter — a composite made by the Great Spirit to foretell the coming of spring.

The bluebird does not adapt well to our urban life; but a bluebird house on a fence post in the country is quite apt to attract them still. Though apparently not as abundant as formerly, they can be seen quite commonly on power lines along country roads. When one learns to recognize their chubby silhouettes or their plaintive two-note call, it is evident that bluebirds are far more common than at first supposed.

Illinois Status: Common migrant and summer resident throughout the State and permanent resident in southern part.

Eastern Bluebird
(7 inches)
(tree: soft maple)

ASIDE from hummingbirds, kinglets are the tiniest of birds — small, fluffy, active morsels which, in spite of their spidery feet and little bodies, seem to thrive in cold weather. The golden-crowned kinglets arrive when winter is about to begin, when the chill breath of January is suspected even in the ruby leaves of October. Among the falling leaves the tiny birdlets flit and squeak, and when the leaves all lie on the ground and, on a deathly silent, bitter-cold day, snow comes to cover them, the kinglets still are here. Among the hemlocks and snow-laden spruces in cemetery and park, the little birds fluff out their feathers until they are roly-poly balls that somehow keep aflame the spark of life. With enough food they find this easy enough, even in below-zero weather.

Small insect eggs and sleeping insects hidden in bark crevices are hunted out with sharp eyes and tiny beak, and with this fuel the body heat is maintained at 110 degrees. The thick layer of underfeathers is fluffed out and so are the outer feathers, to make dead-air spaces which insulate the warm body from cold. The thin legs and feet are tucked up — and the well-clothed bird morsel is contented in a frigid world.

The golden-crowned kinglet has a striped crown and a line through each eye, two white wing bars, and olive-grey feathers. The crown of the male is brilliant orange and yellow bordered with black. The female's crown is pale yellow and black. Look for kinglets in town and park, in woods and cemeteries, birds so small they may go unnoticed until a thin "see-see!" sounds from icy twigs somewhere above.

Illinois Status: May be found throughout the State in fall, winter and spring. Far more common in southern than in northern part in winter, yet its presence is recorded on almost every serious winter bird census.

Golden-crowned Kinglets (4 in.)
top: male; bottom, female
(tree: hemlock)

THE ruby-crowned kinglet is a preoccupied little body without much fear of people. With a fluttering of small wings, a darting into the air for insects, a light-footed skipping among leaves and twigs, the ruby-crown may even come within reach of an outstretched hand, so close that all markings are visible. It is then that a brilliant scarlet tuft of feathers flashes on the crown, subsides, and flashes again with every flittering movement of wings and body, a brilliance that seldom is seen at a distance. The tuft is absent in the female. The large eye is very beautiful and composed, set off with a white ring which gives the tiny bird a charmingly big-eyed appearance. Two white wing bars, an olive-green body — the ruby-crowned kinglet suddenly dashes out of arm's reach, is up and away among the leaves.

The kinglet comes in April, usually before many leaves have appeared on the trees. Here it plays among the redbud flowers, feeds on tiny insects among dogwood and apple blossoms, plucks small worms from new foliage, or, moth-like, hovers an instant to catch a gnat or midge. In May the ruby-crown goes to the North Woods, where in the top of a balsam a large ball of a nest is made of fir twigs, leaves, and fibers. In late summer the kinglets come south again and for a few weeks in September and October once more visit gardens and parks.

The song of the kinglet is something to anticipate, something to treasure for its completeness. This tiny bird produces a finely woven song, a small, powerful succession of sounds, at first only a sizzling but which materializes into neat phrases, and much more, perhaps, that is lost to human ears. It is a song to remember from season to season and to cherish forever.

Illinois Status: Common migrant but rare winter resident.

Ruby-crowned Kinglet
(4¼ inches)
(tree: redbud)

148

THEY were there in the apple trees that morning when April snow unexpectedly covered the world with out-of-season cold and whiteness. There they were, a trifle puffy as to feathers, but exquisite in the morning sunshine as they picked tentatively at the frozen, withered apples that had dangled there all winter. Cedar waxwings, in spite of their appearance of languid leisure and delicate temperament, are hardy birds, and their comings and goings are unpredictable. In the middle of January there may be a softly hissing flock of thirty or so perched in a treetop, or in unhurried fashion eating the bitter high-bush cranberries in the park. Or waxwings may arrive one day when the cherries are ripe, eat their fill, and suddenly depart. In an orchard a pair may consent to nest, but not regularly nor every year. They come and go, an erratic tribe, in search of fruits and berries, and perhaps for some hidden grail which they never quite succeed in finding.

Waxwings and the tufted titmice are the only crested grey birds east of the Rockies. They seem alike, yet are very different, for the titmouse is all nervous energy; the waxwing is unhurried and mannerly. Its feathers are among the most beautiful possessed by birds, are unutterably soft and Quaker-colored, each laid carefully in place. A thin crest rises on the head, a bit of black marks the throat and face; there is a wash of pale lemon-yellow on the breast, an opalescent grey-brown on the back and head. A band of yellow puts a border on the end of the tail, and on the wings there are tiny tips of scarlet "wax" — hence the name of waxwing. Such beauty as this must be enjoyed for itself alone, for the waxwing has no song, only a soft high hissing "cee-cee." Watch for waxwings. They are common visitors in backyards, parks and cemeteries.

When your ear is tuned to this thin high call, you will discover that the cedar waxwing is quite common. As the wandering flocks fly by, their mixed medley is so soft it may be missed even in the quiet open country, yet so distinct that the trained ear will detect it over the sounds of a city.

Illinois Status: Common but erratic birds found at all seasons of the year throughout the State.

Cedar Waxwings
(7¼ inches)
(plant: high-bush cranberry)

IT is summer, and the sun is warm. Insects are everywhere, and in the cornfields where the stalks are more than knee-high, grasshoppers leap and chirr. The shrike, a trim, pearl-grey bird with black and white wings and tail, and a distinctive black velvet mask over its eyes, sits quietly on an osage orange twig and looks in meditation at the ground. The bird is apparently disinterested, motionless, and then suddenly flies straight across the field to a distance of almost fifty yards, hovers, while the wings flash black and white, then drops. The grasshopper, spied from a distance by those keen eyes, is caught in a hooked beak like that of a hawk. However, the shrike has the typical feet of perching birds, rather than the talons of hawks and owls.

With a low swooping glide that carries it close to the ground, the shrike flies back to the hedge, and with a characteristic upward swoop, lands on a twig. At once there are shrill baby-cries from a nest hidden in the thorny fortress. The grasshopper, still kicking feebly, is crammed down the throat of one of five hungry young shrikes.

At another time, perhaps, the grasshopper is neatly impaled on an osage orange thorn and hung up until it is wanted. Sometimes a mouse is kept so, or a small bird, and because of this habit the shrikes are known as butcher birds. Here in the guise of a lovely songbird are the habits of a hawk.

Not that this black-masked, beautiful creature sings often. It reserves that for rare spring moments when, as if it can be still no longer, the shrike mounts to a high twig in the hedge and begins to sing — sings like a catbird or a mockingbird, with innumerable mimickings, grace notes, and original melodies rendered in a powerful tootling voice. The shrike comes here in late winter and stays until late autumn. In midwinter the rarer great gray shrike sometimes is seen. It is distinguished by a finely barred grey breast, by the fact that part of the lower beak is flesh-colored, and by the larger size.

Illinois Status: Common migrant throughout the State. Permanent resident in southern part, a common summer resident in central and less common in the northern part.

Loggerhead Shrike
(9 inches)

THOSE huge fall and winter flocks of short-tailed blackbirds circling around and around in the sunset sky are starlings which, with a dry rush of wings and a shrill chattering, swoop down to trees and building ledges where they roost in unbelievable numbers. They are not true blackbirds though a few of the latter may mingle with them.

Starlings are among the strangest of our birds, foreigners from a distant land. The present generations no doubt have enough American lineage behind to make them naturalized citizens. They came from England in 1890 and 1891 when one hundred European starlings were released on Long Island, purportedly by the same man who was responsible for bringing the English sparrow to our shores.

There were one hundred glossy, loud-voiced, busy blackbirds, and immediately they made themselves at home and began to nest and rear their young in bluebird nests and woodpecker holes whose owners were unceremoniously ousted. Gradually the starlings took over New York City, almost ended the reign of sparrows, and then spread westward. Around 1929 and 1930 when starlings were seen in central Illinois, they were looked upon as rarities. Today, in their enormous flocks they are among the most abundant of birds; and by the late 1940's they had reached the West Coast.

They scatter about town in small detachments in winter — officious busybodies waddling about on short legs and poking a long yellow beak into every cranny of lawn and garden. In summer the starling is black, prettily glossed with iridescence, but in winter it is a black bird amply speckled with small yellow-white spots — truly a freckled blackbird with a voice.

Yes, a voice indeed! The starling normally squeals and shrills at random, but often in spring one lone, loquacious individual may utter portions of the songs of meadowlark, bluebird, robin, wood thrush, pewee, crested flycatcher, or even the tufted titmouse and nuthatch.

Illinois Status: Abundant permanent resident with a habit of gathering in great flocks in late summer, fall, and winter.

**Starling
(European Starling)
(8½ inches)**

WHEN the sunny upland is dry and hot, when vervain and mullein thrive, and a tangle of blackberries blooms and fruits in summer, a bird sings all day long. It is the mystery bird of the hedge, the voice without a body. For years one may pursue that voice, chase it up and down the long hedge and catch only a fleeting glimpse, if at all, of a small grey bird that pauses momentarily to utter a strange, gobbling gabble. And so, pursued, the bird one day poses on a twig in full sunshine. Look well — it'll be gone in a moment. A little green-grey bird with a wash of pale lemon-yellow on the throat and sides, two prominent white wing bars, white around the dark, bright eyes, and a stubby beak. This is Bell's vireo, a bird of the Middle West whose eastern limit lies somewhere in Indiana. It appears rarely in the eastern states, but central Illinois is one of its favorite haunts. Here it sings and nests along country lanes and in thickety places, in upland pasture and thornbush area.

Well hidden in a blackberry tangle is the nest, a neat, small, well-woven basket of fibers slung on a twig only a few feet from the ground. It is such a strong nest that when the leaves finally fall and the vireos have all gone south, the little basket swings strongly in the winter wind, is heaped with snow, or perhaps is host to a deer mouse that appropriates it for its winter nest. And when spring comes again, the vireo basket is still firm and well-woven. It marks such an obviously good nesting place that often the vireos return to the same bush each year; their length of residence is often indicated by the number of empty nests hung about in the bushes.

Illinois Status: Common migrant and summer resident in favorable local areas in southern and central parts but irregular and uncommon in north.

Bell's Vireo
(5 inches)
(tree: osage orange)

ALONG the lazy summer street where elms make graceful arches and the dark shade is pleasant — the leaves are deep green now, and somewhat dusty since the last shower — a voice runs over and over again in the same unvaried song. Somewhere up in the leaves is the warbling vireo, a small grey bird that is whitish beneath with nothing much to distinguish it but the pleasant monotony of its song, one that seems nicely fitted to the atmosphere of lazy summer days. It becomes an inseparable part of summer, of warm sun and deep shade, of luncheons in the garden, of camps and picnics and summer strolls. The sweet, leisurely warble is seldom varied, ending in an upswing just as if a question mark were placed at the end of its song. And then the pleasant little song comes again, repeated over and over all day long no matter how hot the weather.

The warbling vireo is as much at home in city trees as in parks and woods. High in a tree on a resilient twig of the outer branches, a small, woven basket is swung to hold the white, speckled eggs. Both parent birds take turns at brooding the eggs. When the male is serving his turn, he seems to accept the post cheerfully, and to while away the time in the nest he often sings his usual songs.

The red-eyed vireo is the other common vireo of city trees and, like the other vireos, is more often heard than seen. Its distinctive song is a once-a-second rhythmic staccato. In a soprano voice, the red-eyed seems to sing "sweet Marie," first ascending a three-note scale and then descending the same slurred notes over and over all day long. This common little songbird of the big woods and residential areas tends to build its beautiful, suspended, cup-like nest in lower branches of trees, sometimes just two or three feet from the ground.

Illinois Status: Both are common migrants and summer residents throughout the State.

Warbling Vireo
(5½ inches)

LATE in January when the spring call comes to warblers wintering in Central and South America, they begin a leisurely flight to the North, yet keep well behind the reach of northern cold. Slowly they move up the country until by mid-April the first myrtle warblers appear in the trees, and in another two weeks or so, other kinds arrive. From May first to the twentieth the great flood of warblers flows through Illinois trees — through parks, cemeteries, gardens, city trees and woods. Wherever there are trees there may be warblers, tiny birds infinitely varied in color and pattern, different in song and habit, yet all of them warblers. They move incessantly, flutter their wings, and sing their strange, unmusical little songs. They come and go, sometimes lingering until late May, or they may depart hurriedly when a hot spell comes. They like cool, damp spring days, so that in weather of this sort the visitor to their haunts perhaps may see thirty-five different kinds in one morning. Among them, creeping on tree trunks, is that striking pen-and-ink sketch of a bird, the black-and-white warbler.

It runs about on tree trunks and branches in search of tiny insects hiding in the bark, and has been known to nest in central Illinois, though the majority go north with other warblers to Michigan, Wisconsin, or Canada. One other warbler, the worm-eating, has the habit of creeping up trees, but it is olive-greenish with black stripes on the top of the head. Though the blackpoll is sometimes mistaken for the black-and-white warbler, the former is chunkier, is not so cleanly marked, has a black cap, and does not creep on tree trunks.

Illinois Status: Common migrants.

Black-and-white Warbler
(5 inches)
(tree: burr oak)

AMONG the small maple leaves just coming into a chilly April world, or among the blossoming plum trees humming with bees, there comes the earliest warbler of the season, the patchwork myrtle. It is a hardy bird, a warbler with a constitution strong enough to survive late cold snaps and early frosts. The first myrtles usually arrive in the first week in April, though occasionally a few come in March. This is indeed early for a bird that wintered along the Gulf Coast or in Florida.

Then, when dogwood is in bloom on hills along the river, when spring is at its height everywhere, more and more myrtles come until they are the predominant bird. The myrtle warbler is neat and well marked, bluish slate marked with black, white, and yellow, the latter in distinctive patches on rump, crown, and sides. The throat is white, bordered below with black, the sides marked with a long streak of yellow. Even in autumn, when the myrtle returns on its southward flight and has lost most of its spring colors, the yellow rump remains as a definite mark of identification. As late as November it flashes like a signal among the bare twigs. In spring the myrtle eats many insects; in late autumn it is very fond of poison ivy berries, and in coastal and southern states feasts for long weeks on the fragrant grey fruits of the bayberry.

The palm warbler seems to prefer to look for its food in the low understory of woodland and yard, often dropping to the ground to scratch for insects and grubs in the debris beneath the shrubbery. It is the "tail-wagger" of the warblers, flicking its tail with nervous precision as it hops about or perches on a low branch. This tail-wagging habit — along with the brownish back, yellow wash beneath, prominent yellow eyebrow line and bright brown topknot — helps to identify this migrant warbler.

Illinois Status: Both are abundant migrants throughout the State.

top:	Palm Warbler	(5¼ In.)
bottom:	Myrtle Warbler (Yellow-rumped Warbler)	(5½ In.)
		(tree: dogwood)

WHERE willow tangles grow along the muddy river shores, where mosquitoes are shrill and fierce, and crayfish burrow in the mud, there comes the loud, ringing voice of a river bird. Out of the willows darts a flash of intense orange-peel color that gleams in the sunlight, brilliant yellow offset by blue-grey wings, back, and tail. This is the prothonotary warbler whose difficult name might well be changed to river warbler. It is devoted to the bottomland country and is seldom, if ever, found away from it. When other warblers swarm in city trees, parks, and woods, the prothonotary heads for the river shores. Here, in a deserted woodpecker hole in an old tree, the prothonotary lays its speckled white eggs and cares for its young. It is one of the few warblers that nests in the central states, and, aside from this point of distinction, it is one of the most brilliantly colored of our birds —pure color set off by bright black eyes. It is part of the picture made by snaggy dead trees standing in swamp water; of the open stretches of brown river and willowy shores; of the hot, muggy climate of the Illinois summer.

When observed casually, the prothonotary warbler may simply be passed off as a "wild canary," an improper term often used for several small yellow birds, particularly the prothonotary, the goldfinch, and the yellow warbler. Because their chosen habitat is so remote, prothonotary warblers are probably more common than they are familiar.

Illinois Status: Fairly common migrant. Common summer resident locally in southern and central parts. Fairly common summer resident locally in northern part.

Prothonotary Warbler
(5½ inches)
(plant: American lotus)

164

WARBLERS bring a glimpse of the tropics to northern woods in spring. They come and in a few weeks are gone, but their stay coincides with the blossoming fruit trees and pollen-dusted pines, with the snow-effect of spirea and the pink spice of wild crabapple bloom. Among all these blossoms the warblers hunt and devour millions of harmful insects. Yet in spite of brilliant color, quick movement, varied song, and abundance, the warblers are almost hidden in the new-leafed trees and bushes.

But at five o'clock on a scented May morning, when the air is clean and fresh after the night and birds swarm in every tree, the whole procession of warblers passes through woods and cemeteries, through towns, parks and woodlots. There are warblers in almost every group of trees; they sing, flit, fly, and flash bright colors in the May sunshine. It is a pageant which marks the height of bird migration in Illinois, for when the warblers leave for their homes in the northern woods, spring migration is over.

Among these brilliant birds is the blackburnian warbler, a clean-cut black and white bird with gilded orange on head and throat. There are the butterfly-movements of the black and yellow magnolia warbler that spreads and flirts its fan-like tail. Or perhaps the buzzing song of the golden-winged warbler calls attention to a bird with a black cheek and throat, and yellow on crown and shoulders. The warblers are all a lively throng, and a great many which are native to America pass through Illinois in May.

Illinois Status: Blackburnian and magnolia are common migrants while the golden-winged is an uncommon migrant.

top to bottom: Golden-winged Warbler (5 in.)
Blackburnian Warbler (5¼ in.)
Magnolia Warbler (5 in.)
(tree: haw)

THE yellowthroat nests at the marshy edges of water, be it just a roadside ditch, a farm pond or the shore of a great river or lake. It is a strikingly small, lively bird, bright yellow beneath, olive-brown above. Its distinguishing mark is unmistakable — a black mask over bright black eyes.

The yellowthroat is fond of weed patches along the road, trumpet vine tangles in the river lowlands, or overgrown places in backyard and village. With an uneven flight, the yellowthroat bounces in and out of the tall grass and bushes and utters a sharp call that becomes an integral part of the summertime. "Witchity-witchity-witchity," is its nearest approach to syllables — a tuneless song, yet eloquent and expressive. Sometimes the yellowthroat bursts upward from its bush and flutters into the summer air, singing as it goes, a feat which is common though seldom mentiontioned.

The nest, made of fine grasses and plant fibers, is usually near or over water in weeds or willows, sometimes even on the ground cannily set beneath a big shady burdock leaf. Three to five white eggs finely specked with red-brown are laid in the nest. Young birds and females are yellow below and brown above, without the distinctive black mask which is such an excellent mark of identification of the male.

When you learn the cheerful cadence of its "witchity-witchity-witchity-witch," you will realize how very common is this elusive little warbler of the moist edges of natural settings.

Illinois Status: Common migrant and summer resident throughout the State.

Yellowthroat
(Common Yellowthroat)
(5¼ inches)
(plant: spike grass)

ALTHOUGH most of the warblers remain provokingly high in the trees, a few of the more obliging glean small worms and insects from bushes in woods, parks, and gardens. Chief among the ground-dwelling warblers is the ovenbird as it parades among the new fern crosiers and jack-in-the-pulpits. It is a neat green-brown creature with a thrush-like appearance, yet the striped orange and black crown and a peculiar teetering gait identify it as an ovenbird, never a thrush. Its song is loud and distinctive. To some it sounds like "teacher - Teacher - TEACHER - TEACHER!" in ever-mounting crescendos, but to others it is just an enthusiastic, ringing clatter that starts thoughtfully and ends with a shout.

As the ovenbird runs about among the new ferns, other warblers skip about in the bushes and in the trees. Among those that like to stay near the ground is the quiet, big-eyed Canada warbler, a smooth, unmarked blue-grey above and bright lemon-yellow below, with a sharply defined black necklace across the throat, and a yellow ring around the eye. With the Canada may be the tiny Wilson's warbler, a bright yellow and green mite with a dab of black for a cap — a busy, nervous little bird named for the dour Scottish birdman, Alexander Wilson. These are three of the thirty or more species of warblers that add excitement and challenge to the sport of birdwatching during the few days each spring when the migrating warblers pour northward to their various nesting locales.

It was Wilson also, who, so the story goes, found the Kentucky warbler after a long search for an elusive voice somewhere in the Kentucky woods. Today that same bird — bright yellow beneath, brown-green above with a black mark through the eye and down the cheek — nests in river woods and shady ravines. It drops out of the northward migratory movement each spring to nest not only in Kentucky where Wilson discovered it but also in southern and sometimes central Illinois. It chooses tangled, thickety places where it puts its grass nest on the ground, slips among the bushes, and sings a far-reaching, almost ventriloquial, lonely song, a haunting melody sung through all the long hot days of midsummer.

Illinois Status: All are common migrants. Ovenbird may remain to nest in central and northern parts in suitable heavily wooded areas.

top to bottom: Kentucky Warbler (5¼ in.)
Canada Warbler (5½ in.)
Wilson's Warbler (5 in.)
Ovenbird (6¼ in.)
(tree: wild crab)

170

WHEN the yellowthroat is nesting in a weed thicket, and the prothonotary warbler has laid its eggs in an old woodpecker hole near the river, and most of the other warblers have left the Illinois woods, the American redstart begins to nest in the trees of river woods. Many redstarts stay here all summer — a common bird of the floodplain forest — exquisite, flaunting, little "butterfly birds" of the high trees.

The redstart has a fascinating story. The bird may travel to South America three times and back, a distance of 4,000 miles, before it acquires that jet black, snowy white, and flame-orange dress which is first seen in the spring of the third year. The female and the younger redstarts wear brown instead of black, yellow instead of orange. But they all flirt their tails, open and close them like fans, droop their wings to show vivid color-spots, and twist and turn in what appears to be great vanity, but which is just the usual manner of redstarts.

With the redstart on the opposite page are shown two other common migrant spring warblers. The black-throated green warbler's musical rhythmic buzz is one of the more easily recognized and remembered of the warbler songs. It seems to say, "See! See! Look for me!" Over and over in rapid succession the first two clear staccato notes are followed by the three of the last phrase. In dense tamarack and black spruce bogs of the North Woods, this little bird may sing day after day from the highest tip of a spruce tree.

The chestnut-sided warbler is a common migrant in Illinois; and a few stop off to nest in the northern part. Visually, it is distinctive and easily recognized by its yellow crown, white cheeks, throat and chest, and the striking chestnut sides; but its song may be confused with that of the common yellow warbler. If the typical song, "I wish to see Miss Beecher," comes from a dry, bushy, clearing or pasture, look for the chestnut-sided warbler; if from a streamside, city park or farm woods, look for the yellow warbler whose song is similar.

Illinois Status: The black-throated green and chestnut-sided are common migrants. The redstart is an abundant migrant and summer resident.

top to bottom: Black-throated Green Warbler (5 in.)
Chestnut-sided Warbler   (5 in.)
American Redstart   (5½ in.)
(tree: Scotch pine)

YEARS ago when sparrows first were introduced from England, no one considered that they might reproduce in America in such great numbers, or so quickly. Now they have spread over most of the country, have eaten myriads of young grasshoppers as well as young lettuce and new peas, have occupied barn and tree, guttering and gable, have filled downspouts with nests, sidewalks with feathers, and late winter mornings with a quality of music which, though somewhat strained, is often the only song to be heard in town.

When winter closes down with sooty, snowy, windblown severity on city street and backyard, a draggletailed row of sparrows waits every morning on fence or hedge. They eye the back door for possible scraps from the kitchen and are a regular part of the daily birds that dine at the feeding stand. The sparrows soon learn where they are fed and come to wait every morning before sunrise. When the door opens and food is distributed, the door is scarcely closed before the sparrows fly from all directions as if they had been waiting for blocks around and had just received word of new beneficence. They gobble and fight, argue, and try to fly away with crusts as big as they are, and by this exercise at least keep themselves warm.

No other bird has so successfully adapted to the habitat of man. It consumes with enthusiasm an unbelievable variety of food: hard dry seeds, soft pulpy fruits, insects, grubs, worms and almost any food scraps from our tables. Being gregarious, they feed and nest in flocks and are almost always associated with the habitat of man.

Illinois Status: Abundant permanent resident.

House Sparrow (6½ in.)
males, left; female, top right

WHEN a strong March wind blows straight out of the South and brings with it the odor of miles and miles of wet earth, flowing water, mellow old leaves, and swelling poplar buds, there may come a sudden, thrilling song, a carol that seems to come from nowhere, yet everywhere. Here is the silver voice of spring.

The clear melody follows the same pattern over and over again. Perched on a fence post or in a sodden field, a meadowlark is singing. It is a stout bird streaked brown above, but it has the gold of pure summer sunshine splashed on the breast, and a striking black V is painted across it. Down in the grass the lark is difficult to find, so well does its streaky brown and tan coloring blend with the dead grass and weeds. But up there on the post where a pushing south wind ruffles the feathers, the golden front gleams like a buttercup. It is spring, and the meadowlarks are back.

They fly with a sputtering noise and a spreading of white tail feathers and soar on bent wings low over the growing alfalfa or hunt insects among the red clover. The nest is of grass, wreathed around to make a shallow bowl which rests on the ground in a sheltering hummock. Here, in imminent danger of scythe, reaper, snakes, and the other dangers that beset ground birds, the speckled brown eggs are laid and brooded. Soon the first young are grown, and a second and sometimes a third brood is hatched and reared. Meadowlarks sing in the open sunshine all summer long, even until late November when their carolling is like the voice of a spring that has come too soon.

Every niche in nature has its own particular wildlife population, and most of these habitats include birds. The open prairies of modern Illinois, primarily farmlands of corn, soybeans, wheat and forage crops, have been adopted and well populated, particularly by meadowlarks, horned larks and dickcissels. The meadowlark, though the least numerous of the three, is the best known, probably because of its striking, bright song.

Illinois Status: Permanent resident in southern part. Common migrant and summer resident in north and central.

Eastern Meadowlark
(10¾ inches)

176

FIVE birds are harbingers of spring. Usually in late February or by the end of the first week in March, the mourning dove, the bluebird, the robin, the meadowlark, and the redwinged blackbird have all arrived and are singing in the chilly air. In the dead old cattails of pond and swamp where last year's seed heads still fluff out a pale tan down, the redwings teeter and sway — jet black birds with a gloss, and a brilliant epaulet of scarlet and gold on each shoulder. In song the bird seems to exert every effort to produce good music. The tail becomes an eloquent fan; the feathers seem to open; the bloodred patch on the shoulder becomes a living bit of color. And so with all this effort and display, the song comes forth, "O-ka-reee — O-ka-reee," — a gurgling, springtime sort of song, thrilling when it comes for the first time after a long and almost songless winter.

The redwings are back! Brilliant, showy blackbirds of swamp or park pond, singing, singing, blowing in the wind, they wait impatiently for the streaked brown females to come up from the south. When the females arrive, usually two weeks later than the first males, the song and display grows more fervent. Soon a nest is begun in the cattails, willows, or last year's prairie grasses near or in a marsh, roadside pond, farm pond or on a lakeshore, wherever the birds can find nesting places two or three feet above or beside water. Although farm field drainage has greatly reduced the marsh areas, which the redwing prefers for nesting, this bird has continued to thrive and has adapted its nesting requirements even to the little roadside drainage ditch.

The nest is built with the fibers of local plants which are used to bind together the standing reeds of cattails, grasses, and even willows. In these conspicuous bulky nests usually four pale blue eggs are laid. Each egg seems to be inscribed with a cryptic, scrawled, black pattern.

These blackbirds stay all summer in the swamp; in autumn they gather in big flocks in smartweed meadows and lowland marshes where some may spend the winter and be the first to sing in spring.

Illinois Status: Abundant migrant and summer resident.

Redwinged Blackbird
(9½ inches)

IT is cherry blossom time, when crisp white blooms cover black twigs with an unbelievable beauty. An April-blue sky, a fluttering drift of white petals — and suddenly in the midst of all this there is a throaty, heart-stirring carol, a bird of glistening orange-gold and black. April — cherry blossoms — and an oriole.

Few birds are as gorgeous as the Baltimore oriole; few birds seem so much a part of the deep purple gloom of the Honduran jungles, a part of orchid-hung mahoganies, or the bold grandeur of the Mayan temple country. The oriole belongs in a setting like one of these, yet half the year it comes to nest in Illinois trees. Most of its kin are left behind in the South—the golden troupials, the cassiques, the oropendulas — but two orioles out of all the tribe travel northward in spring. They are the Baltimore, named for the ancestral colors of Lord Baltimore who settled Maryland, and the orchard, or garden oriole in rich chestnut and black.

A Baltimore oriole seems to like nothing better for its nest site than a long, pendulous branch of an elm or cottonwood tree where, in breath-taking feats of acrobatic balance, the female weaves a remarkable nest of string and fibers, a thick, firm bag sometimes reinforced with horsehair. Here the white eggs scrawled with black are laid and the clamorous young are reared. When the autumn leaves drift down, the empty oriole nest dangles all winter, sometimes for several years, before the disintegrating fingers of wind and weather put tatters in the oriole's careful handiwork.

There are several common birds whose voices have certain robin-like qualities, particularly the Baltimore oriole, the scarlet tanager, and the rose-breasted grosbeak, though each has distinctive characteristics. But the "Peter - Peter" call that punctuates the song of the Baltimore oriole is its special signature which causes one to turn his eyes to the treetops in the hope of glimpsing this brilliant black and orange beauty.

Illinois Status: Common migrant and summer resident.

Baltimore Oriole
(Northern Oriole)
(7½ inches)
(tree: cherry)

WHEN leaves begin to drift from the trees, when the feeling of autumn is in the air and sunset arrives just a little earlier every day, the grackles gather in big flocks and fill the air with their flight. They come over with a dry rush of wings, a guttural clacking, a swish, and a clatter, and alight with jocular gabblings in the trees of park, woodlot, or city street to spend the night.

These are the common grackles — long-tailed blackbirds with a brilliant gloss of purple and green on heads and backs, and rather startling, cynical white eyes. The grackles are fond of company and usually travel in large flocks. During the day, however, they spread out to forage in garden, lawn, or field, and reassemble noisily at night. In spring, too, they separate, and the pairs hunt out nesting sites, preferably high in an orchard tree or a conifer; tall Norway spruces on farms and in windbreaks are well patronized. Here the nest is made bulky with mud, grass, and straw, and the greenish-blue eggs mottled with cinnamon brown are laid and tended. Soon the adult grackles must find food for the young, and quite often they obtain it from the nests of other birds by robbing it of eggs and nestlings.

Then when the young are grown, it isn't long—in August or sometimes earlier — until the grackles, often in company with innumerable cowbirds and starlings, gather in big flocks that scatter during the day and assemble at sundown for a good, rousing, conversational bee before they sleep. They often chatter sleepily all night.

In flight, the grackles can be readily identified not only by their long tails but by the unusual habit of depressing the center of the tail and folding up the outer edges in a "V." This gives the impression that the tail is being carried vertically like a rudder rather than flat or horizontally as are those of other birds.

The grackle's song is probably beautiful to another grackle, but to the human ear the sound which emerges from this hunch-shouldered figure with its half-spread wings is more like the prolonged protesting sound of a rusty gate hinge.

Illinois Status: Abundant migrant and summer resident. Common permanent resident in southern part.

Common Grackle
(13 inches)

182

THE cowbird is emancipated. By some tricky means of an unpredictable Nature, the cowbird assumes none of the unremitting cares of parent birds — none of the intricate business of nest building, the care and tending of the eggs, the toil of feeding hungry young ones from dawn to dusk. This is all taken care of for the cowbird, whose only maternal duty is to lay eggs in the nests of other birds and let the foster parents do the work. A cowbird doesn't put all its eggs in one basket, but distributes them impartially — perhaps one in the nest of a wood thrush, another in a vireo's nest, one in a redstart's little grass cup, and a fourth perhaps in company with a towhee's eggs. Then the cowbird, its duty done, goes off with others of the family to pastures or fields, where flocks of cowbirds spend all their waking time in feeding, walking sedately after the cows, and doing little else.

And what of those eggs which were laid in the nests of other birds? The wood thrush may simply shove that mottled brown and greenish egg overboard; the redstart may build up a false bottom around the intruding egg and kill its chance for life. But the towhee and the vireo may accept the big egg, brood it, and spend their time in feeding the great, awkward cowbird baby, often at the expense of their own young. The egg of the cowbird usually hatches several days earlier than most other eggs. The intruder thus has a head start on attention and food, and makes the most of it. Frequently the rightful occupants of the nest are stepped upon, shoved out, or starved to death, while the cowbird thrives.

But what of the cowbird itself? The male is our only black bird with a brown head. However, for a short time in the fall, this can be most confusing; for right after the fall molt, the male cowbird appears as an all-black bird. On the head it is just the feather tips which are black; and as they wear off, the undercolor of brown shows through. The females and young are essentially grey-brown birds. Study the head silhouette: the cowbird is the only black bird with the short seed-eating bill of the sparrows and finches. It is most helpful as a consumer of weed seeds and insects; in fact, the food habits of few birds are more beneficial to man than are those of the cowbird.

Illinois Status: Common migrant and summer resident.

**Brown-headed Cowbird
(7¾ inches)**

184

IT is May, and from afar the oak woods have an almost autumnal appearance; closer at hand the color changes from a pastel haze to a host of small, individual leaves, each one perfect, pale, and velvety. They clothe the bare trees as with a veil through which the sunshine easily falls and makes a glow of clear light. Among the leaves are birds from the South — birds singing, flitting, calling.

Into this setting there flies a bird of such consumate beauty, such vivid color, that all else is suddenly lost to view. Only that scarlet bird, that bird of fiᵣe with ink-black wings, is here where other birds until this moment had sung and flown. The scarlet tanager is back, and all else is eclipsed.

Nature rarely uses bright red without attempting to hide it. The scarlet cup mushroom is hidden under a log in the spring woods. The glistening ruby throat of the hummingbird moves too fast to be seen well or captured. The cardinal flower blooms best away from the beaten path. And the tanager, reddest of all, likes to stay in the upper treetops. Yet in May when oak leaves are small, this flash of flame against a spring blue sky is sudden, heartwarming, and momentous.

The female scarlet tanager is as inconspicuous as its mate is brilliant — a soft, leafy sort of olive-green that blends with the foliage and is not easily noticed. Some of the tanagers stay here in deep woods, where in a tree a frail nest of fine, thready twigs and rootlets is placed and the pale bluish, speckled eggs are laid. The song is a hurried, disinterested carol that lacks the enthusiasm of the robin's song and is somewhat hoarser; some think it sounds like a robin with a cold. The call is a secretive "chick-churr! chick-churr!" that calls attention to the tanager even before that bird of flame takes wing through the trees.

Illinois Status: Fairly common migrant and summer resident throughout the State.

Scarlet Tanager (7¼ in.)
left, female; right, male
(tree: pin oak)

THE cardinal is all that is elegant and chivalric among the birds. Its crimson feathers vary in brilliance with the season; the crest on the head rises and falls with the emotions. A smudge of black surrounds the big red beak. The female is an olive-brown personality with coral color on the tail and wings; the beak accents the whole ensemble with brilliant coral. Both birds have that compelling whistle which means spring when late winter drags, a song that is a vital part of sunshine and good living. The dominating song of the cardinal seems to call "Whit-cheer, whit-cheer, pretty, pretty, pretty" over and over again from some prominent perch in the backyard.

Cardinals stay the year around in Illinois, and late in the year they congregate in the bottomlands, often in great numbers, where they feed on greenbrier berries and other leftover seeds all winter long. The brilliance of a cardinal in the snow is a sight long to be treasured — a sight which may be had in almost any backyard especially if sunflower seeds, corn, or cracked chick feed (or almost any birdseed mix) is put out for them on a feeding tray or the bare ground. How strong that beak, how regal and dignified the bird, while the mendicant sparrows sit about and snatch up the crumbs dropped by the feeding cardinal.

Perchance even in the city, if your yard has a thick shrub, small tree or, better yet, a little thicket of shrubbery, a pair of cardinals will build a shaggy nest of grass and rootlets, perhaps lined with strands of grapevine bark pulled from old vines. The brownish-green speckled eggs, and later the chicks, are tended with a nervous, noisy, excited solicitude. The adult cardinals click and flutter with conspicuous excitement with every trip to or from the nest. How any nest can remain sufficiently hidden to safely rear young is hard to conceive. Yet cardinals are obviously increasing in number as they readily adapt to the habitat of man. The cardinal is a southern bird which extended its northern range from the Ohio River Valley to the southern provinces of Canada in the first half of the twentieth century.

No matter where they are, or at what season, cardinals contrive to produce a lovely picture — in snow, in springtime sun, in autumn woods, or in the blossoming locust tree that drips great, scented, ivory panicles of bloom.

Illinois Status: Common permanent resident.

Cardinal
(Northern Cardinal)
(7 inches)
(tree: black locust)

MID-APRIL, and the papaws are blooming. Mid-April, and among the queer, red-brown blossoms there sits the first rose-breasted grosbeak of the season. The warming sun strikes down through leafless trees and catches the color of the papaw flowers, limp as wet silk, and gleams on that splendid black and white finch with its bone-white beak and cherry-colored breast.

Songs are all about in April, but above the jumble of spring melody there rolls a strong, varied warble, the masterful music of the grosbeak which is pleasantly changed a trifle by each individual singer. With the quality of a very mellow robin call, it undulates up and down the scale in a pleasant repetitious pattern. The singing seems to be done without effort as the grosbeak sits in a tree and warbles, picks the newly opened leaves and buds, or takes wing in the sunshine. Then the curious flight pattern suddenly shows—a whirling sort of wingbeat in which the large white spot on each black wing appears to go twirling about. Sometimes the grosbeak sings or gurgles as it flies, and when male or female is taking its turn on the nest, either one will sing a low, patient tune to while away the time. Females of only a few bird species sing; the grosbeak is one of these. Its color-pattern differs from that of the male; it is streaked brown with a white eyebrow, and resembles nothing so much as an overgrown sparrow. When the young leave the frail, thready nest they are similar to their mothers, except that the young males have rose-color under their wings, and, as they mature, acquire the first hint of rose-color on their breasts.

The grosbeak, aside from its beauty, character, and domesticity, is one of the most useful birds to find on a farm. Potato beetles, those pests of the potato field, are well-liked by these birds. During the nesting season, grosbeaks can easily clean out a large garden, and in the city they may eliminate hordes of caterpillars which have infested trees and shrubs. But no food pleases them more than the berries of ripening wild cherries, mulberries, or honeysuckle. At these times, they will join with robins, titmice, waxwings and others to gorge themselves on nature's bounty.

Illinois Status: Common migrant throughout the State and a common summer resident in central and southern parts.

Rose-breasted Grosbeak
(8 inches)
(tree: papaw)

ALL summer long the indigo bunting sits on a twig or on a wire not far from a nest hidden in a bush, and by the hour, on the hottest day, lets its own "illumined being" run over with the joy of summer, of green leaves, of sunshine, and good feeling. The bunting is a small, joyous blue bird that belongs to hot days and dusty roads, to the forest edge or a roadside tree. Its song is a drawn-out warble of couplets, spilling enthusiasm and vigor. A man may be parched and dusty, thinking of anything but birds, when this spritely repetitive song penetrates his consciousness. Here in the heat of a prairie summer day, he will be obliged to listen in spite of his discomfort. The rapid successive couplets seem to fit this phraseology: "Fire! Fire!—Where? Where?— There! There!" On and on it will go in rapid musical gurgling staccato.

This dark blue finch, with an almost blue-black head, is a common bird of the Illinois roadside. It may appear as but a small dark sparrow silhouetted against the sky as it sings from a wire or high branch, telling to all the world that this is its territory. Nearby is probably its mate and nest. Every area of Illinois has its appropriate birdlife; the indigo bunting, the dickcissel and the goldfinch are the three prominent finches that have laid claim to the summer prairies.

Scientists tell us that birds do not actually have blue feathers, that the deep, rich blue of the indigo bunting, the bright blue and purples of the jay, and the brilliant blues of the bluebird are just a phenomenon of light refraction. But what care we? Color is only what the eye sees and, to the sight, an indigo bunting is a lovely summer bird, bright blue from head to tail. The female is brown with a little greenish-blue on the wings. And no matter if that glorious color of the male is actually brown, it is still a splendid thing to see, a definite part of the Illinois summer which no other bird can fill.

Illinois Status: Common migrant and summer resident.

Indigo Bunting
(5½ inches)
(plant: culver's root)

THE dickcissel is a bird of clover field and fencerow, of open, sunny uplands, of wires along the highways; and there an unmusical, enthusiastic song is sung without stint all summer long. The dickcissel is a western bird which has moved across the Mississippi and now makes its home in Illinois. It is seldom found beyond the Indiana state line and rarely in the eastern states. It is characteristic of the plains country, a bird of the prairies and open fields and, unlike most birds, seems to enjoy the blazing sunshine of midsummer. The dickcissel is sparrow-sized, yet marked very much like a meadowlark, with a yellow throat emblazoned with a black V. It has white underparts, a yellow eyebrow, a white streak down the wing and bright chestnut-colored shoulders. Daily in summer the dickcissel sits upon a telephone wire or tall stalk, tail tucked down, throat swelled out, and chants a clattering sort of song a thousand times a day without variation, a rather staccato song, more rhythmic than musical. It almost buzzes "Dick - Dick - Dick - ciss-ciss-cissel," the last part a hurried slur.

Down in the cool shelter of pink clover blossoms, or blue alfalfa, in a vetch meadow or a soybean field, there may be a grass nest where sky-blue eggs are brooded by the female, well hidden by her indistinct markings.

The range of the dickcissels throughout the years has varied greatly. Once they were common in western New York and Pennsylvania, where today they are only casual visitors. Some regions today are losing dickcissels, while others are suddenly favored by this bird of the western plains.

On the present prairie farm fields of Illinois, the dickcissel and the horned lark have become the two most abundant nesting species.

Illinois Status: Common migrant and summer resident in central and southern sections, less common in the north.

Dickcissel
(6 inches)
(plant: sweet clover)

194

A T the time of autumn seeding, when milkweed silks wander over the fields and into town, flocks of goldfinches dressed in the brilliant gold and black of the adults, or the brown and yellow of the young, gather in the weed patches where they nibble milkweed and thistle seeds. When the fat seeds are gone, the silks, released on the wind, are a sign that goldfinches are busy and that summer is definitely drawing to a close.

Goldfinches nest later than other birds. When others are engrossed in the serious business of selecting nest material and laying eggs and caring for the young, the gay goldfinches go bounding about the country, tweeting as they fly in a roller-coaster flight from garden to roadside to pond-margin. In July the goldfinches at last settle down to make a thickly felted nest of plant fiber and thistledown in the thorny fortresses of the thistle plants, or in willows and bushes. Here the small white eggs are brooded, and the young grow up hidden in the ample protection of the thorns. Goldfinches are fond of thistles. They make their nests in the great burgeoning plants, feed their young on thistle seeds, and all winter long, as long as the seeds last, visit the thistle patches for food.

In winter the brilliant black and yellow is changed to a modest brownish-grey with a touch of yellow on wings and rump. The goldfinches stay the year around, finding food in open fields or in the treetops where they feed on nutritive buds. Not realizing that the goldfinch is a permanent resident, many people assume that this brownish-grey finch in winter garb is a sparrow. Recognition of its cheerful flight song, sung on the ascending sweeps of its undulating flight, will give an indication of how common is the goldfinch even in midwinter.

The goldfinch is one of the most widely distributed birds across America from coast to coast. It is referred to as a "wild canary" perhaps more often than is any other of the little yellow birds.

Illinois Status: Common permanent resident although erratic in appearance and somewhat variable in abundance.

American Goldfinch
(5 inches)
(plant: milkweed)

SPRING sometimes sees towhees as early as mid-March, when they sing among the bleached old horseweeds in the bottomlands and scratch about in the late spring snow. The towhee, however, is a bird of the open woods, an elegant creature with some of the most distinctive markings to be found anywhere. Here is a glossy, long-tailed bird, jet black above, the head all black, the breast snowy white, the sides bright russet, the long fan-like tail black with white edges. The female has the same markings, but the black is replaced by a warm brown.

Because of its color and terrestrial habits, the towhee is often called the ground robin; but, unlike the robin, it is usually found in brushy woodland thickets instead of on the manicured lawns of residential areas. This elusive ground bird will tantalizingly keep moving beyond view in the ground cover as one attempts to get a closer look.

The towhee likes the ground so well that it nests there — a grass nest built on or near the floor of the woods, where the creamy, speckled eggs are laid — but in song the towhee likes to perform from the highest treetop. Late in the afternoon the towhee flies in a series of short, indirect flights to the favorite song-perch, and there with head held high, it pours forth a series of loud, throaty whistles. Its song is often interpreted as "Drink your tea-eee." Its call is in two distinctly different parts. The first clearly says "Tow-hee" or "Che-wink"; the second is a rapid musical trill in an entirely different range.

Most of the food is obtained on the ground, and here the towhees scratch like small energetic chickens in the fallen leaves and loose, friable earth, where fine black rootlets are found and pulled out for a nest lining.

Towhees often stay until late October, when they become a pleasant part of autumn leaves, the pungent haze of leaf-smoke, and the glow of orange bittersweet along the thickets and the clearings.

Illinois Status: Common migrant and summer resident.

Rufous-sided Towhee (8¼ in.)
top, female; bottom, male
(plant: bittersweet)

AS a haze of blue leaf-smoke lifts in the autumn air, when there is a hint of changing color on oak and maple, and a blaze of scarlet sumac along the roads, juncos come into the weed patches, parks and gardens from the coniferous forests of northern United States and Canada. During their short northern summer they nested on the ground near some huge, grey, lichen-covered bank or boulder, feeding on seeds and small insects. Then when early autumn called, the juncos came south to spend their winter here. They flash their snowy outer tail feathers in that characteristic scissoring flight as they open and close grey and white fantails. On bleak winter days, juncos with bone-white beaks pick up seeds and small gleanings where one might think no birds could find sustenance. The junco is always distinguished by that white beak, that scissoring tail, and by the slate-grey coat and vest, and white underparts, clean-cut and sharp against that dark slate color of the throat and upper breast.

The junco is a ground bird, fond of the clean and cool air of pine and hemlock forests of the North Woods or the high ridges of the Appalachian and Rocky mountains where they hop and scratch beneath the ferns and lady's slippers. They are equally at home in backyards during the rest of the year, where they will come daily for chicken feed and crumbs put out for them.

When spring is barely approaching yet nevertheless is felt by birds, the juncos break into song. All winter they utter small chirps and twitterings, but on a sunny day in March or April the whole flock warbles and jingles like musical bells. And then, suddenly, they are gone, called to the North, where the cool forests offer a summer home to these trim little sparrows.

Illinois Status: Abundant migrant and common winter resident throughout the State.

Slate-colored Junco (6¼ in.)
top, female; bottom, male

O N those icy days when the mercury skids below zero, and there is a shrill, cutting wind out of the North that blows drifted snow-powder in a flying fringe across road and embankment, there come snatches of plaintive tinkling songs like water running under thin ice. Song, on a day like this? Look in the sheltered nooks, in the weed patches in the lowlands, in places protected from the keenest wind by surrounding banks and hills. Here, where last year's bleached horseweeds offer a dinner table to hungry winter birds, the tree sparrows sway on the white stalks and sing cool, broken bits of song.

From their nesting grounds in the Canadian tundra, land of the Subarctic, these plucky birds come down, often in large flocks, into our northern states where the seed heads of tall weeds reach above the snow. Some of them go as far as southern Illinois where on a cold winter day they may be found busily feeding along a roadside or in a weed patch on a forest edge. As gleaners of weed seeds, they help reduce the weed crop of next summer.

The tree sparrow is known by its reddish-brown cap, streaked brown back, two white wing bars, and the clean white front marked by one distinct dark spot which gives the appearance of a hole in the feathers.

As soon as autumn makes its presence known, the weed patches are again hosts to tree sparrows. Sometimes they are joined by crowds of jingling juncos, song sparrows, and the big, plump fox sparrows with their grey backs and red-brown tails. All of them devour weed seeds and sing when winter is at its worst.

Illinois Status: Tree sparrow is a common migrant and winter resident. Fox sparrow is a common migrant.

top: Tree Sparrow (6¼ in.)
bottom: Fox Sparrow   (7¼ in.)

ALL day long in the weedy meadows and pastures, often along a forest edge, there sings a little brown field sparrow — sings from dawn until dusk, and sometimes even trills in its sleep. Listen early in the morning, and note the pattern of the song. Listen again with the same purpose at noon, and again late in the afternoon. It will be discovered that those series of ringing whistles change with the hours. They vary both in pattern and in the tone quality and during the day are performed with innumerable variations.

The slender little field sparrow is one of the few birds fond of open sun and summer heat, and one of the few that sings in spite of it. The bird is pinkish-brown, with a light breast and a whitish eye-ring, two white wing bars, and a small, pale, pinkish beak which as a distinguishing mark is as prominent as the white beak of the junco or the straight beak of a sandpiper.

At the end of a song the field sparrow goes flitting by an indirect route to a bush or weed thicket. Here in a neat little cup of grass are the small, speckled, pinkish-brown eggs.

The field sparrow belongs to prairie country and is never found, except by rarest chance, in woods. It is often seen along the highways, and the hiker, as he crosses an upland pasture full of thorny, cow-chewed haw bushes, may find several field sparrow nests and their timid, flitting owners.

This inconspicuous bird with its clear chromatic song is a true symbol of the grassland meadows of the Illinois prairie.

Illinois Status: Common migrant and summer resident.

Field Sparrow
(5¾ inches)
(plant: mullein)

THE white-throated sparrow is a nesting bird of northern United States and southern Canada. Here in the balsam-scented woods, among the ferns on some moist, forested hill, the nest is made. The white-throat, however, spends a few weeks each spring and autumn in Illinois; it comes from the silent haunts of deer and grouse to a plebian association with the English sparrows in city parks and backyards.

The white-throated sparrow is well marked for quick identification. A black and white striped crown, a distinct yellow spot in front of each eye, a clean white throat on the males, a smooth, pale grey breast, upperparts streaked brown and black, and two white bars on the wings — that's the white-throat.

It is often joined by the white-crowned sparrow which has a broad white crown. The white stripe on the side of the head does not extend forward from the eye, and the front is a smooth grey. The two sparrows often move south or north together.

And when the wild crabs bloom and scent the air with that incomparable spice that means May, groups of brown birds with black and white crowns come under the crisply pink blossoming trees and scratch among last year's leaves. Here on a moist, rainy day when mist drifts down and clings as rain to every leaf and twig, the plaintive, sweet songs of white-throats become a pleasant part of the scene.

In October, when the scent of old leaves and the haze of leaf-smoke fills the cool air, the white-throats come again. They scratch among the fallen leaves and whistle thin clear songs with broken variations in the fragrant autumn air.

Illinois Status: Both are common migrants. White-throated is more common. A few may winter in southern part.

top: White-crowned Sparrow   (7 in.)
bottom: White-throated Sparrow   (7 in.)
                        (plant: wild grape)

MUSIC — it is the theme of the song sparrow's existence. Perhaps it is a day of zero cold, when weed stalks crackle and break, and the drifted snow is like powder. Gaiety is scant, the wind is bitter, but the melody of the song sparrow is like a precious jewel. Or perhaps the day is one of great and unrelenting heat in mid-July, when even the horseweeds wilt in the sun, and no wind stirs in the dusty leaves of willow or river maple. Yet again the song sparrow performs its brilliant arias oblivious to the heat.

Perhaps it is a night in June, when all the woods speak in whispers, and when, in a flood of white moonlight, birds awake and sing a bit. On such a night the song sparrow is restless. Again and again it rouses itself, chants a broken song, and sleeps again. Yet when January sets crackling white stars in a black sky, and the snow itself is illumination enough for the intense silence of sleeping woods, a tremulous song sometimes rings briefly through the cold willows and the tall calm boles of the oaks. It is the song of that unquenchable singer, the little brown sparrow of the brookside.

The song sparrow claims a willow, a tangle, a thicket or a bush, and spends most of its life in the immediate neighborhood. It is as much at home in city gardens as in the wildest swampland, and creeps like a brown mouse through the grass and bushes. The song sparrow is streaked brown above, has a striped brown crown, and the breast is marked with brown streaks that often converge in one large triangular spot in the middle of the breast. This bird is perhaps the commonest native member of the family. It stays here from June to June, nests close to human habitation, or stays, an aloof water elf, along quiet streams and ponds.

The song, repeated over and over again from two or three chosen perches, is known to more people than that of most native birds. Although it varies greatly between song sparrows of the Atlantic and song sparrows of the Dakota prairies, it always seems to be recognizably similar — with two rather different sounding parts separated by a distinct buzz.

Illinois Status: Permanent resident in southern part. A common migrant and summer resident throughout central and northern sections where a few remain locally in winter.

Song Sparrow
(6½ inches)
(tree: shadbush)

208

THE YEAR OF BIRDS

A DIARY

First Week in January

Cardinals, sparrows, starlings, and downy woodpeckers were feeding heavily until late afternoon. Temperature low, with a feeling of snow in the air. Birds seem to sense the approach of a bitter night and coming snow, and stoke up ahead of time.

Saw a farmer's barn wall hung with dead hawks and owls. The hawks with one exception were marsh, broad-winged, and red-tailed, all of them well known for their excellent appetite for mice, snakes, and rabbits. The owls consisted of one barred owl, and two barn owls, all three of which are mousers and ratters. Apparently there is a mistaken notion abroad that there is a bounty on hawks, owls, and eagles, when in reality it is a violation of an Illinois law to shoot any of them.

Second Week in January

The January thaw has come. There was a bluebird today, first of the year. Very early, though it probably won't stay. On the open lake there were beautiful canvasback ducks, their heads a gleaming copper-red, their bodies white in the morning sun. With the canvasbacks were the duller redheads, and some fat ring-necked ducks, each with a white patch on the side that shone out like a light. As soon as there was open lake water, they all came back.

Third Week in January

A tufted titmouse ate quantities of sunflower seeds today and hid many of them in crevices of bark. A flock of starlings camped in the garden, walked about intently, probing and prying into everything, and ate all the bird feed.

Fourth Week in January

Another cold wave and more snow. In the cemetery hemlocks small birds were feeding on seeds in the tiny, rose-shaped cones. These birds were much like goldfinches, were streaked, and had yellow in the base of the tail; they had a different sort of secretive attitude, however, not found in the forthright goldfinch, and a rough "zhreee-zhreee!" call. Pine siskins from the Far North. Severe weather often brings them to evergreens.

First Week in February

How quickly the weather can change! Down to zero one day,

and a few days later the ground thaws and spring is in the air. The birds must feel it, too, because today the first robin greeted the dawn with clapping wings and loud, impatient cluckings. No song yet.

Second Week in February

Robins on the lawn, and soft maple blossoms above. Bluebirds in the park; redwings caroling in the old dead cattails of the pond. A meadowlark spreading its white tail feathers and singing the gladdest sort of song on the windswept golf course. These first arrivals usually come at the same time, and what a thrill they are! Almost no later birds afford the same sense of pleasure as the sight of bluebirds, robins, redwings, and larks on a blowy day in mid-February, when at any minute the temperature is apt to tumble back to midwinter. These earliest arrivals spend the winter only a short distance south in Kentucky, Tennessee, and northern Mississippi. Some of the robins spend the winter in the river bottoms of Illinois.

Third Week in February

The first flock of grackles arrived, with a scattering of cowbirds. Rusty blackbirds were off by themselves, their white eyes and short, square tails distinguishing them from other blackbirds.

Fourth Week in February

Horned larks were flying in a scattered, loose flock all day, even over town. Their high, tinkling calls were almost unreal up there, the birds so high and small they were difficult to see. Horned larks act very much like the English skylark, especially in spring. The males mount high in the sky, singing, and then drop down again to the muddy fields. The scattered flight is a common occurrence in very early spring. They will nest soon.

First Week in March

More meadowlarks, more robins, more bluebirds on every fence post, and grackles clattering all night. Even the house sparrows are attempting to sing, and the starlings almost burst themselves in imitations and caricatures of other birdsongs. They would be almost good if they weren't so smug.

Second Week in March

A woodcock in the Sangamon bottoms. The first phoebe, its tail twiddling, sat on a wire near a culvert beside the highway. It seems early for an insect-catching bird, yet for a week the insect-catching cricket frogs have been awake and singing in the ponds. There is an almost deafening chorus of frog voices in marsh and pool. A song sparrow, usually quite loud itself, makes no headway against such a chorus.

Third Week in March

A kingfisher and a green heron were both waiting for fish beside the park pond. There were many jumbled songs in thickets near the water, where juncos, getting ready for their departure to the north next month, kept up a constant sweet tinkling and a flitting of white tail feathers. With them were tree sparrows, red caps bright and white fronts marked with a single black spot. Their neatness makes the song sparrows and the big ruddy fox sparrows seem almost untidy. The latter two are bespattered in front with brown streaks and spots. The thoughtful songs of the fox sparrows are lovely now.

The lake was alive today with ducks and their enemies. The white gulls swarmed; pintails, shovelers, mallards, American widgeons, gadwalls, teal, and scaups were peppered over the lake. Above them soared eagles — three magnificent adults whose white heads and tails, in contrast to dark brown bodies, gleamed at a distance with four other eagles, all dark but very large — immature birds. There were ospreys hunting fish and two speedy duck hawks harrying the ducks. When one of these ferocious bullets came racing low over the water, all the scaups laid low, and in a fright went paddling away as fast as they could manage, but the duck hawk was only playing and swerved up again.

Mourning doves were cooing heavily all over the cemetery today. Wonder how long they've been here. Many doves come very early, others not until mid-March, but even then they begin to look about, in their futile, vapid, dove manner, for possible nesting sites.

Fourth Week in March

The first day of spring, dark grey and cold, with a chill wind out of the north and a feel of snow in the air again. This morning, however, a flock of Canada geese went north, and there was no doubt after that that spring was really coming. What is it about wild, honking voices in the sky that strikes a chord deep inside a person? A heartbreaking nostalgia for something — something far away in the goose country, perhaps, and unattainable. Flying geese arouse a feeling almost of despair, a longing for wings, a sadness, yet an exultation, too. Today the first geese went north, and there will soon be others.

The day after spring, and there was snow last night. A deep, quiet, very, very wet "robin snow," and this morning every blade and twig was inches deep in crystal. The birds didn't mind very much, not even the horned larks that undoubtedly had eggs in nests beside the fields. The horned larks sang, and the meadowlarks puffed out their feathers and sang, too, from the fence posts, a little doubtfully at such a turn in the weather. The first thin, sweet whistle of a field sparrow was unexpected on a day like this. Purple finches, most of them sparrow-like, with one strawberry-red

212

male among them, nibbled elm buds and warbled snatches of throaty song. Birds in the weed patches were jocular — they'd seen snow before — but the puzzled towhee kicking up snow as it scratched in buried leaves, as towhees do, apparently had never seen the stuff in its life. By noon most of it had melted; now perhaps spring will really stay.

Fourth Week in March

The first great blue heron came to the lakeshore. In the woods the first myrtle warbler made its appearance — very early, for they aren't due for another two weeks or so. They spend the winter in Louisiana and along the Gulf Coast, and arrive ahead of other warblers. But March — that's really early for a myrtle warbler!

The first hermit thrush. As the sun came into the moist, misty bottomland woods the birds were already singing, and a hermit thrush perhaps felt something that reminded it of the North Country, because it broke its usual migration silence and let fall a magnificent, heart-stirring series of liquid notes. It is easy to see why the hermit thrush has become so famous and so much beloved. There is a quality in its notes that sets it apart from all other birds and songs.

First Week in April

The first brown thrasher woke the dawn and began a medley of twice-repeated calls and grace notes. It's really spring when the thrashers come.

With them are purple martins, gurgling as they cut curvets in the air. Ruby-crowned kinglets in the bushes, vesper sparrows beside the road, green herons by the pond. A small, energetic, bobbing winter wren in the bleached old horseweeds beside the stream. On the lake still are many ring-billed gulls, but they are scattered now. At anchor on the water are multitudes of scaups and mallards, with detachments of blue-winged teal and mergansers. There are groups of widgeons in the inlets—grey ducks with white caps— and a few grey gadwalls with russet shoulders and white patches on their wings. Canvasbacks and redheads are still here.

Today a great blue heron flew on slowly flapping wings north over the Capitol Building.

Yellow-bellied sapsuckers in the park, meowling and tippling on fermented maple sap in previous borings on the tree trunks. Violets, bluebells, buttercups, and toothwort in bloom in the lowland woods.

Second Week in April

Today there was a strong melodious tootling song somewhere up in a tree, a loggerhead shrike, a carnivorous songbird that seldom sings, now doing its bit to make the April morning merry. Only by chance is it heard to sing.

The first palm warbler, singing a high, new sort of song and with every breath energetically twiddling its loose-jointed tail. More myrtle warblers — in fact, myrtles are becoming so common one grows tired of seeing always them and no other members of the family. White-throated sparrows were piping and scratching in the garden today.

Third Week in April

The lake is full of interest now, as it has been all winter. Common terns are here, with the very similar Forster's terns, and the businesslike black terns, all beating up and down the lake. There is nothing else like the gaiety, the complete and masterful flight of terns. Even the gulls seemed stodgy beside them.

A big black and white osprey swooped down to the lake and rose with a scream, a big red carp wriggling in a stern and relentless grip of bluish claws. The bird rose high and circled, the fish held lengthwise like a pontoon on a seaplane.

Fourth Week in April

Coots along the lake. Spotted sandpipers teetering and bobbing on the shore. Chimney swifts darting through the air. Bank, rough-winged, barn, and tree swallows everywhere, chattering throatily. A nighthawk early this morning called in the noise and turmoil of a brief thunderstorm before dawn. More new arrivals — least flycatcher, upland plover, solitary vireo, warbling vireo, black-throated green warbler, house wren, ovenbird, black-and-white warbler. In the woods a whip-poor-will rose from a log where it had been sleeping and fluttered off with a moth-like, floppy flight.

Scarlet tanagers and the green females were everywhere in the park this morning. They sat here and there like strange, brilliant tropical flowers in the newly leafing trees.

The first hummingbird dashed about the columbines in the garden. The first prothonotary warblers are clattering by the river.

First Week in May

More new arrivals everywhere, coming thick and fast. Every night they come in, and when morning breaks they are everywhere, fluttering in the trees, in the bushes, or running on the ground. Catbird, wood thrush, solitary sandpiper, great crested flycatcher, kingbird, Baltimore oriole, orchard oriole, bobolink, indigo bunting, rose-breasted grosbeak, red-eyed vireo, yellow-throated vireo, Nashville warbler. A yellowthroat sputtering in the bushes; redstarts in the bottomland trees; a veery singing reedily from a tombstone in the cemetery. These are all here by the end of the first week in May. The yellow-breasted chat, Bell's vireo, wood pewee, and yellow-billed cuckoo quickly follow.

Second Week in May

Swainson's and gray-cheeked thrushes in the garden. White-throated sparrows still remain, one junco among them, a leftover. Will it stay all summer?

Wrens were cleaning the debris from their nesting box today. A golden-winged warbler drank daintily from the bird pool at 5 a.m. The trees in town are full of clattering Tennessee warblers that must have dropped in after a long night of flying.

Parula warblers, yellow warblers, a worm-eating warbler, yellow-bellied flycatcher, Cape May warbler, blackburnian warbler. The Bewick's wrens were splitting their throats today in inimitable song and went poking and prying about the brush pile.

Robins are nesting — again.

More warblers overnight—the bay-breasted, blackpoll, Wilson's, and Canada. Short-billed marsh wrens clattered in the marsh. Semipalmated plovers, like miniature killdeers, in the swamp. Here also were yellowlegs, solitary sandpipers, semipalmated sandpipers, and a single stray western willet. Redwings and meadowlarks are nesting. Several pairs of shy blue-winged teal may stay here to nest.

Field sparrows are nesting. Eggs are already laid in the little grass nests on the ground.

A few cormorants remain on the lake. Most of the ducks have gone, and so have the gulls. The lake, lately so well populated, is strangely empty.

Third Week in May

It was very hot yesterday, and this morning there is scarcely a warbler to be seen. A half dozen big blackpolls, which usually stay late anyway, and a lone Canada warbler were all that remained of the migrant warblers. There were the yellow warblers, of course, and a singing Kentucky warbler, redstarts, yellowthroats, a yellow-breasted chat, and a high-up cerulean warbler, but all of these stay here to nest.

The hot weather cleaned out most of the migrants. The tanagers are gone, and so are the migrant thrushes, the kinglets, many of the vireos, the white-throated sparrows, and the terns. The tree and fox sparrows left long ago with the juncos.

It is an empty woods, somehow, with full-grown leaves and the settled feeling of summer, and yet it is not empty at all because of the nesting and song that continue.

Robins are very busy feeding their young. Bluebirds already have young out of the nest, and the horned larks lead their half-grown infants into a world in which roads are dusty and the fields are growing. Flickers are very noisy and spend their time in digging huge holes in trees, yapping and bowing and dancing ridiculously on telephone pole or tree.

Fourth Week in May

Catbirds are nesting in the lilac bush; thrashers are in the syringa thicket and come sizzling out with yellow eyes blazing and wings spread when anyone comes near. The first young robins are out on the lawn, almost as large as their parents that feed them, but distinguished by spotted breasts and babyish actions.

A whirring and a squeaking in the fireplace chimney indicates that the swifts are nesting there again. A little agile twisting of one's head, with due caution for a shower of soot, and one may look up the chimney and see a little saucer-nest plastered against the chimney walls, and perhaps a bird or two clinging to the bricks.

First Week in June

There are nests everywhere, if one could only find them. Yet it might be better for them if they went unfound. A curious fox, peering from its hiding place at a passing human being, watches to see what the man-creature is up to, sees him find a nest and go on. Then the fox may follow the trail and very neatly rob the nest. Snakes may follow where human feet mashed down a trail through the grass and find the field sparrow's nest. Hawks may observe from on high. Crows and jays are always on the lookout. All in all, it is safer for the birds if interested human beings don't try to find the nests. Most, however, are so well hidden that it is a feat to find them. They are seldom noticed until the leaves fall and show mocking, empty nests dangling in the wind.

Second Week in June

A Traill's flycatcher was sneezing in the willow thicket today. Must be nesting here. Young screech owls must be out of the nest. Out in the garden this evening we were assaulted by a wrathful owl that clicked its beak most alarmingly and dashed down with beating wings almost on top of our heads.

Third Week in June

Robins are out of the nest again—what, again? We scarcely had noticed that nests were being made, and now here are the young again.

Fourth Week in June

There must be young orioles near, though the nest is well hidden somewhere up in the poplars. A continual squeaking and complaining is indicative of orioles. The young rose-breasted grosbeaks complain, too, but in a very polite way. Three fuzzy youngsters with pink under their wings sat in the cherry tree all day long saying "Here? Here? Here?" as a gentle reminder to father and mother that they were hungry.

Often well-meaning folk try to rescue these babies and get into difficulties with the food problem. Young birds seldom fall from their nests before they are able to get about. When they are out of the nest, nothing will keep them in it again, and besides, the parents are usually nearby somewhere and feed them regularly. They do a very good job alone. Anyone who has undertaken the job of feeding young birds successfully knows what an unremitting and thankless task it is. Young birds are perpetually hungry.

First Week in July

Today a nest full of chimney swifts fell down into the fireplace where the parents could not reach them. The babies were too small to climb back up, though their big, rough "elbows" looked as if they had already scrambled about on the bricks.

At 4 a. m. when the sky is still dark, there comes the morning chorus of robins, a tide-like chorus that begins somewhere at the edge of things and rolls over town in a flood of robin song as the sun rises. At this hour, apparently, every male robin feels it his duty to sing. When the thrashers, catbirds, martins, and other early birds begin, the robins slack their efforts and, their duty done, cede the field to the others.

Second Week in July

Hot, and the birds feel it. Only a few sing during the day, except for those that carol at dawn. But neither heat nor nesting cares can silence the songs of the sun-lovers, the dickcissel, the indigo bunting, the field sparrow, the grasshopper sparrow, the song sparrow, and the yellow warbler. Bell's vireo gabbles in its thornbush; the warbling vireo sings in the upper trees; the pewee wails in the heights of the woods. Most birds feel the heat, and go about with their mouths open. In hot weather this is as much a necessity to the birds as perspiration to the comfort of a human.

Third Week in July

The bird pool now needs refilling twice a day or more. It evaporates quickly and is used for many baths and drinks from early morning until almost night. The birds seem to stand in line, and great is the impatience of the bath-loving catbirds when a plump robin occupies the pool, sits in the middle with feathers fluffed out, and just soaks for ten minutes or so. Sometimes a line of sparrows sits meekly around the edge of the pool to catch a shower of drops splashed up by the bathing robin, catbird, thrasher, or cardinal. How they all love water! And spray from the hose these blistering days is a luxury quite worth the cost of the water. Dozens of birds come from all around to splash in the fountain.

217

Fourth Week in July

The first egrets arrived at the lake today — pure white wings flying against the dark muddy shores and the woods behind: it's good to see these southern visitors again. They are reminiscent of sights in the Everglades, along Bayou Barataria, in the Combalue Swamp, or in the Avery Island Sanctuary in Louisiana. Egrets are abundant in all these places, but perhaps no more so in late summer than they are here in Illinois. Small snowy egrets are scattered among the larger kind. It is fun to watch the former scrape with their yellow feet in the mud and perform a sort of dance to stir up fish and crayfish.

First Week in August

The goldfinches are finally nesting. They are the last birds to assume household and family duties. About time, too!

A bird slipping quietly through the leaves turns out to be the first of the returning migrant throng from Canada. A greenish pine warbler — and now the backward flood moves south.

Second Week in August

Again as in May there are warblers in the trees, but they are far more difficult to see or identify. Now the leaves are very thick and dense, and the birds, clad in inconspicuous fall plumage or in the undecided patterns of young birds, are shyer and harder to see.

Third Week in August

Flocks of sandpipers wade along the mud flats and in the green algae-slime below the spillway of the dam. Large numbers of least, semipalmated, and spotted sandpipers are here, with a noisy rabble of killdeers disputing everything with the whole assemblage.

Fourth Week in August

On the wires and bare trees along the river and its swamps there are thousands of tree swallows. They sit like notes of music on a staff, side by side, neat and dainty. Occasionally one flies into the air to snip an insect, or a whole detachment from a section of wire takes wing, swirls about for a few minutes, and returns to the wires. A pleasant, throaty chattering is all about. When the swallows gather like this, it means that autumn is really near.

First Week in September

More warblers in the trees and flitting through the cemetery. This is a fine place to see birds, well protected, quiet, and full of big trees. A big barred owl that lives in the bottomland woods nearby flew out of a thick spruce where it had intended to spend the day in sleep. If these owls weren't so easily startled they would seldom be seen. They are probably commoner than they are believed to be.

Second Week in September

A solitary vireo was hunting insects in the garden locust tree today, and a Swainson's thrush ran about in the wild flower bed, scratched like a little chicken in the leaves, and pecked the fallen seckel pears that lay on the ground.

Third Week in September

The woods really look like autumn. Sassafras is burning orange and red; maples are yellowing; elms are gold; sumac is brilliant along the roads; and oak seedlings, well in advance of their elders, are vivid with reds and purples. Bittersweet is beginning to pop open, and wahoo seeds are bright. In a tree is the first yellow-bellied sapsucker on its way south.

Fourth Week in September

Along the hilly country road the hazel brush is pied with many colors and the sugar maples, each one different, are scarlet and pink and orange. Quantities of yearling sparrows fly up in flocks along the roads and dash into weed tangles and fields. At this particular season they do a great deal of good in devouring weed seeds and late insects.

Today against the intense blue of the sky a flight of hawks went south. Red-tails, Cooper's, and marsh hawks, the latter sailing low over the fields, the others soaring high in vast circles that kept them moving southward. A masterful flight — a strength of wing, a grace of body, a poise that meets air currents with ease — hawks are splendid in their own free element. Captive, they are tragic.

First Week in October

The first returning juncos, chippering as if glad to be back. With them are the first golden-crowned kinglets, brown creepers, and white-throated sparrows. In weed patches along the roads are many birds — tree, song, fox, white-throated and white-crowned sparrows, with many cardinals, purple finches, Carolina wrens, and an occasional downy woodpecker hammering valiantly against the cane-like stalk of a big horseweed. The air is chill today, but the roadside birds are very active.

Second Week in October

As sunset dyed the park pond, a little pied-billed grebe swam about and dived repeatedly in that pool of liquid color.

Now large flocks of cormorants drill up and down the lake and far inland when sunset nears. They make even better formations than geese — tremendously long V's and slow, precise wingbeats.

219

Third Week in October

The first mallards and black ducks are gathering on the lake. A scattering of ring-billed gulls adds sparkle to the day, which is grey and chilly with a hint of coming cold. The gulls dip and fly against the wind, balance on its currents, drop down often for a shining hickory shad, and squeal eerily in the crisp air.

Big flocks of grackles, with a scattering of redwings, cowbirds, and starlings, fly from somewhere late in the afternoon, and either go somewhere else, or camp in the neighborhood trees.

Fourth Week in October

Suddenly many birds are gone. There are no more nighthawks or swifts, no more swallows. The orioles left in September, the hummingbirds with the first frost, rose-breasted grosbeaks and indigo buntings in late September; the cuckoos, vireos, warblers, thrushes, wrens, thrashers, and catbirds, one by one. There are still occasional myrtle warblers and ruby-crowned kinglets. And there are still robins and meadowlarks and bluebirds and redwings and doves—the birds which came earliest in spring are among the last to leave.

First Week in November

Nights are cold now, and most of the color has left the trees. Last night, however, was damp and rainy, with very low clouds. The geese were heard long before they came in sight — a loud, wild clangor somewhere in the moist darkness. From a downtown street they were plainly visible, large flocks picked out in silver from the lights of town. Silver-bellied geese flying against the clouds, moving from one formation to another, and honking — honking with those hoarse, thrilling voices that make Canada geese so exciting. Apparently they were confused by the reflected light on the clouds and circled above town for half an hour until they got their bearings and flock after flock headed off into the darkness.

Second Week in November

Doves are flocking. Great flocks of mallards and black ducks, with a scattering of pintails, hooded mergansers, buffleheads, ruddy ducks, green-winged teal, and common goldeneyes have gathered on the lake. By this time there must be five thousand, by next week ten thousand. An osprey has been seen over the lake for a week or more.

Third Week in November

A wonderful flock of snow geese and blue geese came down on the lake on their way south from Baffin Island to Louisiana. It is unusual that they stop—it's supposed to be virtually a nonstop flight. A thrilling sight indeed! Blue-grey bodies and white heads for the blue geese; pure white with black wing tips for the snow geese. There are big grey Canadas in an inlet farther south on the lake, and a few that are much smaller, probably the Hutchins's goose.

Fourth Week in November

The annual Thanksgiving bird hike. Here were the familiar winter birds — the tree sparrows twittering, cardinals flashing bright red, woodpeckers hammering, brown creepers picking on tree trunks, flittering juncos beside the path, a nuthatch head-down on an oak. A chickadee upside-down, too, and having a merry time of it. Cormorants sitting like snakebirds on the water. One lone loon in winter plumage far out on the lake. And about a million ducks, mostly mallards and blacks. The lake is peppered with them. The gulls, too, are delightful, all ring-bills—white wings against grey sky and greyer water.

First Week in December

Short-eared owls were flying about this afternoon over fields beside the highway. A queer, moth-like, silent flight — long white and golden-brown wings, a small body, and a gnomish round head with yellow eyes. They came so close that even the color in their eyes was visible. It seems odd to see owls flying in daylight, but these apparently liked it and, when they wearied, they perched on telephone poles.

Second Week in December

The first snow, light, soft, and gentle. All last night it fell, and this morning there were flocks of horned larks, the northern kind with their yellow eyebrows, and Lapland longspurs walking in a dark, compact flock through the snow-heaped stubble. A big grey marsh hawk beat slowly and precisely over the field, so low that its wings almost touched the ground. It covered the entire field, quarter by quarter, and then flapped off to try another.

Third Week in December

Birds come abundantly now to the feeding stand — many sparrows, of course, but other birds, too. The sparrows are there even before sunup, the other birds only a little later. To the cracked chick feed there comes a daily quota of cardinals that today numbered ten individuals, six females and four males. They were lovely in the snow. Goldfinches came in their duller winter plumage; tree sparrows look for buckwheat and millet in the feed; titmice and chickadees, juncos, and blue jays all eat mixed seeds and corn. To the suet tied on a tree trunk, downy woodpeckers, brown creepers, titmice, and chickadees come daily. Yesterday a leftover flicker, puffed up with cold, gobbled great bites of suet, but failed to return today.

Fourth Week in December

One day this week folk throughout the country take their annual Christmas bird census conducted by the National Audubon Society (See *Audubon* magazine for further information). The census may be taken on any day in a stipulated period, but the day after Christmas is somehow an excellent time for it. Start early, not too early by the clock, however, because most birds don't stir much until the sun is up, and it doesn't rise until after seven in December. Hunt for birds all day, list them, count numbers, and come home tired but happy late in the winter afternoon. The following list of birds was seen one Christmas bird census in the vicinity of Lake Springfield, not a large list for May, but exceedingly satisfying in December.

Temperature 45 degrees in morning, 20 degrees by night.

Wind southeast, increasing by night and changing to northwest.

Weather cloudy and damp, colder and snow by night.

Lake and river open.

Double-crested cormorant, mallard, black duck, (of these two ducks an estimate of 10,000 was made), pintail, green-winged teal, redhead, ring-necked duck, lesser scaup, common goldeneye, ruddy duck, red-breasted merganser, sharp-shinned hawk, Cooper's hawk, rough-legged hawk, sparrow hawk, bobwhite, ring-necked pheasant, coot, ring-billed gull, screech owl, barred owl, kingfisher, red-bellied woodpecker, red-headed woodpecker, downy woodpecker, hairy woodpecker, northern horned lark, blue jay, crow, chickadee, titmouse, white-breasted nuthatch, brown creeper. Carolina wren, mockingbird, robin, golden-crowned kinglet, starling, house sparrow, cardinal, purple finch, slate-colored junco, goldfinch, and song sparrow.

The Last of the Year

The cold which came rushing out of the North on the day of the bird census sent the temperature down to five degrees above zero, with deep snow. Yet today in the park a small tin-horn sort of voice announced the red-breasted nuthatch, denizen of mountains and the Far North, brought here by the cold. There was a big blue goshawk in the pine plantation and an eagle over the frozen lake. The year's at an end, and the cold weather brings fine things that presage much that is good in the year to come.

INDEX TO BIRDS